The School of Travel

The SCHOOL *of* TRAVEL

TWENTY YEARS *in* CENTRAL EUROPE
(Croatia and Czech Republic)

Donald (Donny) N. Roberson, Jr.

NEW YORK

LONDON • NASHVILLE • MELBOURNE • VANCOUVER

The School of Travel

Twenty Years in Central Europe (Croatia and Czech Republic)

Published in New York, New York, by Morgan James Publishing. Morgan James is a trademark of Morgan James, LLC. www.MorganJamesPublishing.com

Proudly distributed by Publishers Group West®

Scripture quotations taken from the (NASB®) New American Standard Bible®, Copyright © 1960, 1971, 1977, 1995, 2020 by The Lockman Foundation. Used by permission. All rights reserved. lockman.org

Morgan James
BOGO™

A **FREE** ebook edition is available for you
or a friend with the purchase of this print book.

CLEARLY SIGN YOUR NAME ABOVE

Instructions to claim your free ebook edition:
1. Visit MorganJamesBOGO.com
2. Sign your name CLEARLY in the space above
3. Complete the form and submit a photo
   of this entire page
4. You or your friend can download the ebook
   to your preferred device

SBN 9781636983516 paperback
ISBN 9781636983523 ebook
Library of Congress Control Number:
2023948021

Cover Design by:
Rachel Lopez
www.r2cdesign.com

Interior Design by:
Christopher Kirk
www.GFSstudio.com

Morgan James
PUBLISHING

Builds

with...
Habitat
for Humanity®
Peninsula and
Greater Williamsburg

Morgan James is a proud partner of Habitat for Humanity Peninsula
and Greater Williamsburg. Partners in building since 2006.

Get involved today! Visit: www.morgan-james-publishing.com/giving-back

"The Road Not Taken" by Robert Frost

Two roads diverged in a yellow wood,
And sorry I could not travel both
And be one traveler, long I stood
And looked down one as far as I could
To where it bent in the undergrowth;

Then took the other, as just as fair,
And having perhaps the better claim,
Because it was grassy and wanted wear;
Though as for that the passing there
Had worn them really about the same,

And both that morning equally lay
In leaves no step had trodden black.
Oh, I kept the first for another day!
Yet knowing how way leads on to way,
I doubted if I should ever come back.

I shall be telling this with a sigh
Somewhere ages and ages hence:
Two roads diverged in a wood, and I—
I took the one less traveled by,
And that has made all the difference.

Contents

Preface

This autobiographical book details how I spent almost twenty years living and working in two countries, Croatia and the Czech Republic. It includes activities while I was working, details on Croatian and Czech culture, people I met, and some of the different topics I learned during this time. I have found that travel is like going to school. I entered into the "school of travel," took a variety of classes, and tried to incorporate the lessons I learned. I know there are many of you who enjoy reading about travel and experiences in other cultures. To this end, the purpose of this book is to recreate my time there as accurately as possible. This was done with the hope that you will perhaps be inspired to travel, to meet other people, and to get to know the great big world that is our home. And maybe this will lead to more understanding, peaceful interaction with others, a better knowledge of geography, and even a personal transformation. I have also placed the book within the idea of travel as a school—something from one of my previous research papers, called *Learning while*

Traveling: The School of Travel. I am presenting the idea that travel is like entering a school, with teachers, classes, recess, and the bully on the playground. The educational theme is mentioned throughout this book.

Because I lived abroad for twenty years, this book also includes several of the travel experiences I had in other areas. All pictures in this book were taken while I was there unless noted. Please note that I am writing from personal experiences, and if I have made some errors or if something should be said in a different way, please send me your comments. Everything related in this book is true as far as I can recall. I include various "scenarios" reflecting the wide range of adventures awaiting the traveler. These are scattered all through the book randomly. There are also several descriptions of people I met throughout the book, and there is a continual reference to school, as a way that travel can educate the traveler. When you travel somewhere, it is not a continuous experience; you will encounter many varieties of people and scenarios each day within that particular trip.

Europe is full of beautiful churches with grand architecture and imposing heights, not only in large cities but also in small rural areas. This church is in Sternberg, Czech Republic, a town of about twelve thousand people.

Chapter One:

What Makes a Traveler?

W alking over to my neighbor's house, I knew that once inside I would see things differently. There were three boys there, whereas at my home, I was the only boy. They used powdered milk and mixed it with the regular milk. And they went to a different church and prayed touching some necklace around their neck. For me, all of this was interesting.

Another friend's house had a completely different smell. Also, there was a dog inside the house, running, barking, and adding to all the excitement. His mom made a special toast from a pound cake. For me, all of this also was interesting, and I was fascinated by the different ways people lived. I liked it all and wanted more!

Once a year, our parents loaded us into the car, and the five or six of us would go on an adventure to Daytona Beach or the North Georgia mountains, and even one long trip to Washington DC with our next-door neighbors, the Perrys. It was all very friendly, happy, and enjoyable. Every day was positive with the potential of adventure and excitement. Although I was bubbling over with enthusiasm at each turn, I could look around and see others did not feel the same.

I often wonder why some people never leave. Some folks never go on a trip or even leave home. One of my uncles would say to me, "I don't need to go anywhere, and you are just wasting your time, running all around." And there are others who can travel but won't because of endless excuses. "Well, I don't have anyone to go with me." Or "Who is going to feed the dog?" Or "I am not sure it's safe to go there." Or "I can't drive that far." What is going on inside our heads to make us cancel our trips? Why do we shun subways, airplanes, cruise ships, strangers, or foreign countries? What makes others venture out? Who will go on these adventures, and who are the dropouts and why?

Although, the joy of being at home is also a treasure. The sense of completeness you can feel and the lack of need to travel can also bring a sense of satisfaction. I remember one of my aunts saying, "Donny, I don't need to go anywhere; I have seen all I need to see. I am just happy to be here." I thought, *How wonderful that is*; and one day, I too will be there. But I am not talking about that perspective now; rather I am talking about the inability to travel, make new friends, see new places, or greet new ideas.

This is a book about travel, about the way travel is a school, but it does not have to be over the ocean. It can be next door if we are willing, if we are curious, if we will listen. I invite you to join me in the world of travel and to join the school of travel.

Ibrahim

Fall of 1997. I met Ibrahim while we were involved in some Christian activities in Bosnia, in a town called Tuzla. I was there with Campus

Many of the towns in Europe have areas in the center, without cars, and where the pedestrian can freely walk. Although one must park and walk, the experience of freely meandering around the statues, cafés, shops, and restaurants is very nice. Here is the famous center of Olomouc, Czech Republic. In the background is the town hall, and in the foreground is the famous UNESCO-designated statue, which the town built in thanks to God for stopping the plague. And, if you look closer, you can see my brother and mom walking there.

Crusade for Christ (now known as Cru), and we were sponsoring a class in conversational English, just to help people who knew some English to practice with native English speakers. He was in my group. He was very friendly, nice, and athletic, and he was interested in talking with us. He is one of the few Muslim folks I have met. I asked him if he would like to go bowling and we went. After our class, we exchanged contact information, and I tried to keep in touch with him. We visited this area several times, trying to help strengthen churches and make friends with students. When I returned, I would contact Ibrahim and we would meet. He became comfortable with me, and since his family had a car, he wanted to drive me around the area. He began to share things with me slowly. "Donald, this is the area where I was forced to fight when I was a teenager during the Yugoslav Wars." He showed me various places where he was involved during the war. He explained more about his faith to me. Ibrahim discussed what it meant to be Muslim, and I asked a few questions about his faith. Like many others in this area, he grew up Muslim, like many in the USA South grow up Protestant; however, during the war, most of these somewhat nominal Muslim people became more convinced of their beliefs. I eventually met some of his family and friends.

We kept in touch, and when I was in Sarajevo after 9/11 (the Twin Towers attack in New York City), I contacted him, and he was surprised I wanted to meet him after all the backlash against Muslim people. We met for coffee and had a nice talk while smoking a "hookah." (This is a very typical Arabian pastime in coffee shops.) This was almost ten years after our first meeting. Ibrahim has become a medical doctor and specializes in brain surgery.

Chapter Two:

Meditate, Think about, Consider . . .

Most of us are eager to share about our travels or to explain to others the joys of our journeys. We have all had to endure the history of the captured moment, from slide shows to movies to videos to photo albums, and now the mobile phone is jutted into our vision, uninvited, to show us enchanting photos, adding more fuel to the mystery of travel. Most of us have folders, baskets, or drawers full of photos we have never put away, or mobile phones or data clouds full of repeated photos of costly sojourns. If you have this book, I venture to say you like to travel, maybe love to travel. I would like for you to take the Travel Test and begin to think about your travels.

Travel Test
Please be as honest as you can when you answer the questions in the Travel Test.

1. Describe a travel experience. When? Where? Who? What? Interesting travel details? Who organized this trip?
2. If you repeated this trip, what would you do differently?
3. What are your main memories from this trip?
4. What did you learn while you were on this trip? Also, what did you learn about yourself or others?
5. What are the positive experiences from this travel?
6. Were there mistakes made during this trip or negative experiences (from yourself, others, or service providers)?
7. Did you meet or have meaningful interactions with any local people during this trip?
8. What were your approximate expenses on this trip? Was this experience worth the money paid?
    a. Transportation
    b. Accommodation
    c. Food and drink
    d. Entertainment, program, or museum
    e. Souvenirs
    f. Other
9. Anything else you want to say about this trip?

(Travel Test is a part of research sponsored by Donald N. Roberson, Jr., PhD. You can reach him at dnrobersonjr@gmail.com)

What Makes Travel Meaningful?

Meaningful travel occurs when one sees the important aspects of one's life within the framework and contrast of another place or culture. One lady I interviewed as part of my research said, "To be able to see and to know the people, the dedication of some of them . . . to their church . . . to be able to have that firsthand experience of two different churches in Kenya. . . ."

In addition, meaning and impact in travel occur when there are inter-actions with locals. ". . . He kept getting closer and closer . . . and looking at my skin . . . he was fascinated with my tape recorder. . . ." Rather than becoming enmeshed with other travelers, often these travelers reached out to locals and attempted to make contact with them.

Learning in travel occurs as a result of preparation before and after the trip. ". . . I appreciated the whole world because I did a lot of read-ing about things . . . about the world, geographically, and the people, buildings, . . . just that I got to see it more, made me feel more akin to it, and that much more amazed. . . ." Also each person in this research discussed the importance of effective tour guides: ". . . We felt safer with him . . . we could ask him anything, and he could answer it for us . . . we felt close to him. . . ."

This anticipation of the trip often results in planning and prepara-tion that may last a year before the trip, and it often continues for a year after the trip as they continue to learn more about the places they visited. This excitement of an upcoming trip adds a new meaning and signifi-cance to the person's life. One couple discussed how much they enjoyed reading about places they were going to visit during car trips; another couple discussed how they will continue to read about a location for a year after they have been there. This learning based on actual experiences solidifies their learning.

Of special interest seems to be "surprise learning." This unanticipated response to something new seems to remain in the traveler's mind, forc-ing them to realign previous thoughts and ideas.

Travelers sometimes change as a result of a trip. They identify a change in meaning that can be internal or external. For example, one person states, "As a result of these trips, *I have a wider world*, new friends, new ideas, and challenges." Travel in foreign countries may bring poten-tial troubles on the road. Learning to handle language, money, directions, and location may present a "shallow" disorienting dilemma. Although not a life crisis, each traveler discussed how negotiating these difficulties has resulted in a greater self-confidence and learning. Each traveler discussed similar changes, how they became more confident and more aware of the world.

Sharing Your Trip

Social media can be a great way to share about your trip. Instagram, Facebook, TikTok, or others can offer an easy platform for sharing your story with those who want to hear it. When you return, those who are interested in your trip will ask you to share. There are some who will say, "Wow, I see you went to Paris. Tell me, in a minute, what was the best and the worst part?" And then you may have the luxury of a friend who will sit down with you and really listen as you share your story. Knowing how to respond to the various reactions of a sought-after trip is important.

Scenario. Summer of 1998. Once, while in France, I got stuck during travel because there was a train strike for over a week. I was staying at one of these alpine inns in the Pyrenees, and I needed to get to Spain. I stood up during one meal and explained my situation. One timid man said, "Sir, you may ride with us by car to San Sebastian, Spain; we are leaving in the morning." On this same trip, I noticed we were going to pass through the town called Lourdes. In the Catholic tradition, this is a very holy place concerning Mary. Europe is so influenced historically by the Catholic culture, and I had noticed this name before and thought, *Okay, this South Georgia Protestant can stand some of this.* But I was not prepared to see such a large number of people in search of anything about Mary. There is a cave there where there was a vision of Mary. To get into this cave, there is a long line, and there is water flowing from there, which people come from across the globe for its healing. There are hospitals there. I saw ladies from Italy in some dress of which I can hardly describe, with large tiaras and black veils and long elegant black dresses, lying prostrate on the floor. There are many places around the world, including Forsyth, Georgia, where there have been visions of Mary and which has in turn created its own unique travel culture.

I recommend a few pointers that have worked for me: (1) Choose a social media platform and post your itinerary or two pictures per day. (2) When you return home, offer to give a program at one of your public places, such as your church or local library. (3) Be prepared for the one-minute speech, or the supposedly hurried individual who only wants the best and the worst of the trip. (4) Make a twenty-picture photo album of some photos, bring it with you, and offer to show it if someone asks. (5) While you are on your trip, chronicle your daily activities and write a postcard for each day or location. (6) Use Roberson's Travel Test to write about your trip.

Chapter Three:
Different People

Scenario. After a few years of living in Olomouc, Czech Republic, I began to notice small bronze plaques on the sidewalks. I was usually in too big of a hurry to notice or read them. Eventually, I stopped at one. There was a name, a place, and a date. Someone explained, "So Donald, this is something new, a memory of the Jewish race that was here in Olomouc. Here is the house where they lived, the name of the family, the date and place where they were killed." I was in shock and horrified that I was walking in these places where such horrible crimes had been carried out. I had noticed the absence of synagogues, and I had learned that most synagogues had been destroyed by the Nazis. I have been to Auschwitz, a three-hour drive from Olomouc, five times. Each memorial for me is now a reminder of a regime that I cannot believe existed. Sometimes you will notice a group of these bronze plaques placed on the ground in front of some new building or hotel. For me, they became sort of a small altar, a place for thoughtful prayer, and a reminder of the terrors that people are capable of.

Meeting Different People

Sometimes at your school, you see or are around some different people. These are people different from you, your parents, and your friends.

The Roma—Gypsies—are everywhere.

How can I write this without sounding racist to someone? I try not to be racist; however, I am a social observer, and one cannot escape seeing the issues of social interaction around them. I know it is important during travel and living in other places to learn from these various situations.

At first, I could not understand the issues of "Gypsies." Since then, I have learned the better way is to call Gypsy folks, Roma, or Romani. When I would somehow come across an area where Roma lived, I would see such a wide range of conditions—from abject poverty to wealth. But most of the ones I saw were either poor, or they wanted to give the impression they were poor. Many times they were living all together, in some isolated building, or group of flats. Usually, they were living in dire places and without most normal conveniences. I would see the Roma as I was riding my bike or in my car going somewhere; yet I never really met one. Surrounding their homes was always a large collection of things. It looked like an ongoing garage sale. But, for me, it was fascinating because I had never seen a Roma person except in Europe. Many of them have darker skin, but I have seen all shades of colors with the Roma and even folks who look like me.

One of the first situations I encountered with a Roma person was during the summer of 1992 in Bucharest, Romania. There was a group of Americans who were all part of a Campus Crusade for Christ (Cru) summer project there. Every day, we would go to eat at the well-known Bucharest Hotel. This place offered the best food we could find, and when we arrived, we were often greeted by a group of Roma children who somehow knew of our regular attendance, and they were all begging. They were all so cute, precious, and sweet, holding their hands out, and we were just not used to it.

In another town and country, Belgrade, Yugoslavia (at that time), in the late summer, it could get very hot, and I can remember outside the Moskva or Moscow Hotel, the nicest one in Belgrade, there was a beautiful fountain, a large one, with cool water. This day, the place was full of Roma children, jumping, playing, laughing, and splashing in the fountain—they may have been living

Often when we passed a scene like this, we just glanced and quickly walked by. We knew the parents were nearby and were watching out for their child from afar. But we were captivated by the young boy's charm, music, and smile.

on the streets, but you would have thought they owned the hotel. Their joy and spontaneity were inspiring for me, and I wanted to join them.

Fall of 1993. In Zagreb, Croatia, when I lived there, I saw much more. Children on their own sitting on the sidewalk with a broken arm or other disfigurement, or with something written attached to them, standing there so sweet and innocent begging for money. Healthier ones were sent directly into restaurants and would look for tourists. They would begin this little tapping on your shoulder, and they would not stop until you gave them something. Many times, I would be sitting with people I had met, we would be having a nice meal, and there would be some tapping on my right shoulder. I would turn around and see this amazing, beautiful child, smiling at me, and holding out his hand. He would be very quickly "shooed" away by locals or the folks working there. Around Americans, who were tourists, it was almost funny to watch their reaction, from shock to sympathy, and no wonder the Roma kept returning—there was such a reaction. One of the most common sights would be young women, teenagers, who were nursing a baby and begging for food. You would see someone breastfeeding their child, cradling their baby, and their other hand would be extended to you asking for money with a forlorn look. I saw Roma fathers carrying children in their arms, walking through traffic at stop lights knocking on the windows and asking for money.

Some of the more bold and creative ones would get on the trams, which were often full of people. They would have some musical instruments and would begin playing, and they'd ask you to pay them something for their musical entertainment. I was completely taken in; I enjoyed it, and I was dazzled by their boldness, yet never gave them anything. The longer I lived in Europe, and the more I became part of the society, especially within the academic and education society, I kept wondering, where are the Roma? I never saw one at the university. I never saw a Roma child playing on a sports team. It was a strange phenomenon, and one without many answers, and something for which I could never get an answer. "Donald, you don't understand, the Roma are their own; they belong nowhere, and they have their own rules." I never saw someone mistreat a Roma; however, they were overlooked and not included in society. Frankly, I never understood it, but regardless, the Roma always seemed to be a happy lot living their own unique life.

I was on a bus once riding from Arles, France, to a coastal town in France, and it was about a ten-dollar ride. Everyone paid, except for the Roma. I thought, *Wow, such independence, such avoidance of normal payments, yet taking advantage of what others are using.* It seemed they felt they had a right to all that we had, but without having to pay for it. And they felt they had a right to take your money or something of yours.

Some of the happiest people I ever saw were in the middle of Tuzla, Bosnia. A town wrecked by war and the clash of three cultures, and yet the Roma were surviving in the middle of all of this. In the middle of this small town, where they were living in some shambles of a building, which had been in the middle of war, I heard such a commotion coming from their quarters, and such laughter, music, and happiness was exuding there, and I thought, *God, give me such happiness and zest for life in the middle of such shambles.*

Shockingly, I saw in the market of the same town, mischievous Roma children running around and causing trouble. One of their favorite tricks was to light small firecrackers and throw them at very old people! I would be in a perpetual state of shock and wonder as this little cute boy of four or five would walk up to a man who resembled your grandfather, slouched over, with a cane, simply trying to bring home a bag of bread. All of a sudden, this old man would be turned into the most amazing moving "manikin" trying to shake this firecracker off his arm or shoulder or away from his bag. Similarly, a woman resembling your great-aunt, carrying all the signs of an older body, and as made up as possible, would be moving as carefully as she could through the park, wrapped in shawls. She would be a perfect target, and they would sneak up behind her and put a firecracker in one of the folds of her clothes. They would all be standing by pointing and laughing, and I wouldn't know whether I should laugh, cry, or make a citizen's arrest.

I had many interesting conversations with Europeans about the USA and our life. They liked to point out some of our difficulties and problems. For some reason, they enjoyed pointing out some of the things they heard, such as problems in the USA with race. I would listen and discuss with them. But, when I would bring up the issue of the Roma, their exclusion from society, poverty, or lack of participation, they would say, "Donald, you do not understand." And I still do not.

Learning to Trust

I learned as a result of previous research that travelers can have several basic learning experiences during these adventures. These can be described as learning about self, learning about trust, learning about the world, and learning about home. Those who learn the most are not just going on excursions during allotted vacation time; the ones who learn the most are the travelers who spoke with passion and clarity about learning experiences during these various adventures.

For example, travelers return home with fresh ideas, thoughts, and perspectives. This cognition is often new and empowering knowledge about self. Eating, living, moving, and thinking in a variety of situations will teach the sojourner novel lessons about themselves that prove more valuable than choice souvenirs. This empowering learning about self seems to be focused on the details of travel, seeing others in new cultural backdrops, as well as seeing the self in new contexts.

A simple trip to another country can evolve into a personal discovery of dependence; the traveler realizes the importance of trusting others. Leaving personal details and issues in the hands of others can create trust, safety, and confidence in the traveler. Travel, especially travel in a foreign country, is fraught daily with confusing details of unknown information. An itinerary may depend on the negotiating of mysterious directions and making decisions about undecipherable information. In foreign countries, because of the lack of a common language, the traveler learns about trust in a variety of situations. Traveling out of the safety net of one's home can put the traveler in experiences of difficulty, hardship, and even danger. The wanderer will have to learn to trust; this trust may involve themselves, others, or their God. Regardless, there is a stepping out into the unknown, and this inclusion of trust can offer comfort and hope in dauntingly overwhelming situations. This is especially true of those who are traveling on their own.

When I first came to the Czech Republic, I had a difficult time meeting others and feeling at home. It was not a friendly place to strangers. I was not sure whether I was going to make it there, and I had begun to make plans to leave. I was teaching one class with PhD students, and I was honest with them. How different life was here and that I felt alone. I asked them whether they wanted to do some activity with me, and told them that I would be happy, and that I would be glad to visit them in their hometown and meet their family. There were about five of them who took me up on this. I visited their homes, met their grandparents, saw where they went to grammar school, and learned more about their life. During these situations, we became closer friends, and I began to feel more at home. This unique class began to meet for social gatherings and became closer.

Dagmar

Dagmar, called Dasa, pronounced Dasha, was a student in a class I had for PhD students. She was very bright and energetic, and eventually we became friends. She invited me to visit her home to have dinner with her family, where she showed me some pictures. There was one of her in England. She had worked there, like many young Czech folks, and was a "nanny" for a family. At her home, I met her mother—the father lived elsewhere—and her two brothers lived just yards away. It is in a rural area of Moravia, about a one-hour drive north of Olomouc. They sort of have a family compound there in this small village near the Morava river. Her mother served me baked rabbit—my first time eating rabbit—and it was very good! Dasa was very kind and helpful to me in any way that I needed. After she became a PhD, she got a job as a medical researcher; she is coordinating research projects for a pharmaceutical company. Eventually, she and her husband had twins; one of them was diagnosed with Angelman syndrome. This has occupied their life, trying to help their daughter to become stronger and overcome the difficulties of this. Dasa is an expert now in this particular illness. Like many of the university students in this area, she was smart and creative enough to learn many of the things she needed to know to advance herself and her country despite all of the difficulties in this area in the last one hundred years. Her life has been complicated by having a child with a disability; however, the other twin, her husband, and their new home are also indications that they are moving on and doing the best they can.

The real travel experience—entering the home of the ones who live there, eating their food in their kitchens, listening to their language. Thanks, Kudlaceks!

Chapter Four:

Positive Aspects of Traveling

Scenario. July of 1994. On a bus to meet my team on the Croatian coast, it was extremely hot. No air-conditioning and most appallingly—no windows open. It was stifling, smelly, and simply miserable. However, around me were older ladies all in black, head covered, simply looking ahead as if all was right in the world. We were driving the road along the Croatian coast with pristine views of the turquoise Adriatic. On the right were scattered islands in the distance, and on the left was a beautiful mountain range, the Velebit. I was entranced by it all. Yet, I thought, *If I don't get some air, I will . . . ?* So I got up and figured out how to lower the window and let in some blessed air. Instantly, there was a bus full of clucking tongues, shaking heads, and wagging fingers. I did not care anymore; I was willing to risk their anger, and I needed some heat relief. (For some reason, they think air blowing on you is not healthy.) In another situation, I was sitting in the Jarun park in Zagreb with some friends, and locals were constantly coming up to me shaking their hand. Index finger up, rest of the fingers in a fist, and shaking it back and forth, pointing to the ground. I could not imagine what was going on. One of my friends told me the locals believe you should never sit in direct contact with the ground. "Just put a towel under you, Donald!"

Travel away from the familiar and home puts the traveler in situations that they do not have to encounter while around their home. Travel becomes like its own place of learning, a school, which has the capacity to teach us many lessons.

Good Situations of Travel

The kindness of strangers. September 1993. I was on this whirlwind trip through western Europe before I started to work. I had one more day in Paris, and I had stored my things in the train station in Paris where I would leave for an overnight trip to Barcelona. I went happily on my way to visit places in Paris. I had a picnic on a bench somewhere near Napoleon's tomb and then left for one more place. When I arrived at that museum, I did not have my "zip pocket," with its significant content, including the key to the locker where I had stored all I had. I quickly returned to the Napoleon's tomb area and talked to a policeman. He led me to the police station. Behind some brass bars, I could see my zip pocket lying on a desk. I pointed to it and asked for it. I only had barely enough time to get to the train before it left. The small zip purse was with a note from another person, saying that they had found it and returned it to the police, hoping I would find it.

Two interesting travel experiences that turned out really well—One, I had been on a whirlwind of a trip in Croatia, and I was staying with a family from Hvar, in Bogomolje, and they took me to the end of the island where I had to catch a ferry to the mainland. Bogomolje is a small village in the middle of the island Hvar—a pastoral stone village, very old, with sheep and olive groves. We were staying in their ancient family home, older than my country! (The elder of the family liked to say that.) It was a special time, and I thanked them for this adventure. Eventually, I needed to go, and I was trying to get to the mainland, and then on to Dubrovnik. They drove me to the end of the island where I got on a ferry boat of passengers to the mainland. From there, I walked up a hill to the main highway that goes along the Croatian coast to a bus stop. I knew when the bus would come by, and I walked from the tiny port up the hill to the coastal road. I was sitting there at some bus stop. It was taking much longer than it needed to. So I began to consider what to do. It is about a two-hour ride to Dubrovnik. Several buses came by, and I was waving at them, but they didn't stop—so I began to hitchhike. Time after time, people turned me down, but finally a car full of young ladies from Sweden picked me up and took me the entire way, the two hours to Dubrovnik. They were kind and helpful and refused to take any money from me. God bless nice and kind people during travel.

One more. On the way back to the USA one time, I was riding on the bus to the airport with a friend and her husband where we all were staying. I was enjoying talking with them, and all of a sudden, I was at my little motel, Modre Hostel. I said, "Bye," grabbed my suitcase, got off the bus, and went into the motel. When I registered, they asked for my passport, and I looked around, and somehow during the conversation on the bus, I had put my book bag, or backpack, under the seat of the bus and completely forgotten it. There was money, my passport, and other essential things in it. I took a breath and relaxed, thinking, *I must have the passport, but if it does not show up, then I will stay here until the embassy opens in two days, and I will get a new one.* But I was sure my backpack was on the bus. We tried to call the city bus company, but that did not work. I prayed while walking around the area. I tried to organize my room. Then I saw a taxi drive up, and out came my friends, Josip and Lanie, with my backpack, and Lanie said, "I knew you were praying," with a big smile on her face. While traveling, don't get distracted and keep important documents near you, especially your passport, tickets, and money.

On a trip with my mom. Here we are inside the cathedral in Vienna—
St. Stephen's. It is a massive building with many beautiful windows
and sculptures. You can see the joy of travel on her face.

The culture of Europe. Another "good" is to be able to experience culture in Europe—opera, symphony, ballet, museums, concerts, and beautiful buildings. In the typical town in Europe, usually there are two or three main areas to see, the main church or cathedral, the center of the town, and an art museum. However, if you are living there, you are able to become much more involved in the culture scene of Europe. In my town of Olomouc, which had maybe one hundred thousand people, there was a symphony, a ballet company, and an opera company. These were separate businesses, each one trying to make a profit. Ballet, orchestra, and opera, each one had its own managers and staff, ticket office, and people who promoted the events. There were hundreds of people involved and this was their work. Every week, there were usually two or three choices of these shows, and they were amazing to be involved with. If you can visit one of the larger cities of Europe, such as Vienna or Prague, you will have a choice of these shows almost every night. This has turned into big business. If you visit Prague, you may be accosted by folks dressed up like Mozart, trying to sell you a ticket for a concert. So avoid these "tourist traps," and go directly to Tourist Information for information about the actual symphony, opera, or ballet of the town you are in. In old Europe, there was the tradition of the opera, and through melody and drama, the stories usually were about romance, death, or comedy. Always in a different language, usually Italian, and if you are lucky, there may be a translation in English,

but don't count on it. That is why I settled on symphony and ballet: no words, just beautiful music, and with ballet, amazing athletic skill. These shows can be expensive, maybe twenty-five to seventy-five dollars a seat, but many of them offer a standing ticket, where for five dollars you stand in the back. (Yes, I did this often.)

In Vienna, I loved to attend the symphony at the Musikverein, or Golden Hall. This is a shockingly beautiful concert hall. But rather than pay fifty dollars to sit, I would muster up the strength to

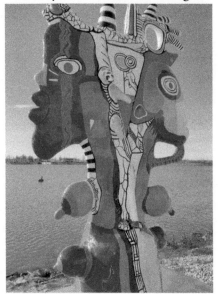

Pictured here is part of the Danubiana museum, a contemporary art museum directly on the Danube River out from Bratislava, Slovakia. In the summer, you can take a boat to the museum and also have a ride on the Danube.

stand in the back. And, not only me, but there would also sometimes be two hundred people standing in this small area in the back of the auditorium. The scene was fascinating to watch; the eager followers of this music would push their way to the front of the area, where there was a rail, and tie some scarf or piece of clothing, claiming this was their spot. Sometimes after an hour or so, some folks would begin to sit down, and in the very back, there would be clusters of children, or teenagers, sitting in circles, with adults trying to get them to be quiet. I realized to stand in one spot for two hours was a great athletic endeavor, and I came out with only spending five dollars.

In the Vienna State Opera, the standing ticket has taken on a life of its own. Every opera offers about two hundred standing places in the very highest part of the opera house. People will begin to line up at 2 p.m. to get these tickets. I noticed that some of these people were regular attenders of the opera, and they knew what they were doing. Some brought food, some brought a portable chair for sitting, and others brought books or knitting. The doors would open about 6 p.m. for the stand-up ticket, and after two hundred were sold, the rest of the crowd was turned away with disappointment on their faces. You would ascend about six flights of stairs and sit or stand in these tiny little places, and the stage way below would look like a matchbox. Once when I was there watching the ballet, *Swan Lake*, when it was over, you would think you were at a rowdy football game; the roar of the crowd was deafening, and there was curtain call after curtain call.

The nature of Europe. Being an outdoors person, I am especially affected by what is out there. I am a big fan of national parks and was interested to see theirs. In contrast to the USA, Europe was already full of people and all of the land was accounted for. So, national parks had a similar, yet different idea. You would see farms, houses, and businesses in national parks. And, unlike the USA, the most beautiful parts of Europe are mostly private or owned by the local governments.

*One of the many walking streets in Vienna, Austria—a capital city, and one
with the rich heritage of the Austrian-Habsburg empire. I was always amazed at
how many people lived, shopped, and went to school in these crowded cities.*

The Adriatic Sea, which is between Italy and Croatia, is a beautiful
area. Off the coast of Croatia, there are almost 1,000 islands (1,244 to be
exact). And there is a large mountain area, the Velebit, which goes right
to the sea. Most of the area is limestone, so beaches are rare; the water
is seven times saltier than the Atlantic, and it's a beautiful shade of blue.
This caused a serious shipping business to develop, and most commerce
takes place between these ships, as well as public travel. Many of these
islands look as they always have, with special stone architecture and very
old buildings and churches. And the locals are a unique group, often
speaking different dialects from island to island.

The mountains of Europe, particularly the Alps, especially those
located in Switzerland, are amazing to see. One of the most beautiful
areas is the Lauterbrunnen Valley in Switzerland, which has the famous

mountains, the Eiger, the Jungfrau, and the Mönch. There are even villages that do not allow cars, only small vehicles that farmers would use. If you go hiking in Switzerland, you will often walk through a farmer's pasture next to the cows with bells around their necks. I can remember one farm in Switzerland where you would ring a bell if you wanted to buy a glass of fresh milk.

Learning while Traveling

How do you learn while traveling? Participants in my research described travel as enjoyable, exciting, and fun. Also, the learning is structured between new and old information, serendipitous and deliberate situations, and simple and complex topics. Furthermore, the findings indicate the learning is situated within a community of learners and is focused on a particular goal. For example, someone traveling through the islands off Croatia is excited, so they are taking in and also learning about the geography of the area. There are new and surprising situations that augment the learning, as well as previous books they have read about the area, plus new information in front of them. And, if they have a question, all they need to do is ask another traveler. Once they are home, they realize they have accomplished a goal—that of learning more about the history of the Croatian islands. (Roberson, Donald N., Jr. 2004. "The Nature of Self-Directed Learning in Older Rural Adults." *Ageing International* 29(2): 199–218.)

Chapter Five:
Learning to Travel

S cenario. Somewhere in Belgrade, Serbia. I have to go to the toilet, and there's one up ahead, a WC that looks different from anything I have seen before. Inside, two women are feverishly cleaning this and that; I see some money scattered around a countertop, and I go on to the bathroom. I walk out and this woman is right behind me hollering something. I can't imagine what she is doing; she is walking up to me with her hand out and pointing to her palm. Basically, in this part of the world, you pay for the public toilet, and there is someone working in each toilet cleaning them. I thought, *Okay, things work differently in some places.* Oh and by the way, you have to buy your toilet paper before you go, from the lady. That was a lesson learned very quickly. I also started carrying toilet paper with me.

Entering the School of Travel

Within the "school of travel," acquiring knowledge during travel experiences is encouraged by normal, even mundane aspects of travel, such as negotiating how to get from A to B, gaining information about different cultures, seeing places for the first time, and interacting with other travelers. There can be a significant amount of learning that takes place during one's free time! One of the most popular ways people prefer to spend their free time is traveling. Travel may create a "perfect storm" for a torrent of learning. You have the chance to learn about yourself, your home, your travel companions, and of course, the places you are travelling to.

Independent tourists move in a small group, they must think for themselves, and they often will take risks during their trip. This forces them to concentrate in different ways than tourists who are following a tour guide. When in a large tour group of fifteen or more, you can get lost in the group, become bored with the style of the guide, or be distracted by fellow travelers. Traveling away from home forces travelers to become closer and form a temporary travel family, thus creating a safe space for travel. Travel, and especially international travel, may result in *enhanced skills* that could be useful in a variety of situations, such as planning, organizing, adapting plans, and dealing with other cultures.

The independent sojourner is hard to find, looks for inexpensive ways to tour, and wants to blend in with the local scene. The tourism industry seems to assume that tourists want top amenities such as four-star hotels, taxis, first-class seats, and signature luggage. In contrast, the independent tourist often sets aside the luxuries of tourism for other desires, such as having authentic experiences, avoiding the crowd, or gaining an education. Tourism does not have to only focus on profit; it can also promote learning throughout one's trip.

Today's tourist is interested in more than relaxation or escape; many are looking for authentic experiences. One way that tourists are improving their experience is through the use of tourism guidebooks. These books are increasing in number and have even become bestsellers in the last two decades. Some of them have launched their own tourist "industry" such as *Let's Go* (www.letsgo.com), *Rick Steve's* (www.rick-steves.com), and *Lonely Planet* (www.lonelyplanet.com). It is a common sight today to see a tourist with a guidebook in their hand. Now, this is quickly changing, as many tourists are simply downloading information or connecting with some local devices through the internet and everything is on their phone.

My entry into the school of travel occurred in 1987. I was working with a Christian organization focused on helping students. It was enough to focus on the needs of people in my country, helping high school students and college students grow in their faith. However, one man working in our organization, Tom Hinkle, was often talking about Yugoslavia. He was encouraging others to come with him for various outreach programs to students in Belgrade, then capital of Yugoslavia. I had never even heard of Yugoslavia and certainly would never have considered going there—I was happy in my summer work at Yellowstone National Park and my regular work with students at the University of Georgia—but he continued.

His persistence eventually entangled me. Tom was enthusiastic, a visionary, and always positive about central Europe; he designed a trip that was hard to turn down. I really had no excuses. On this trip somewhere around December 1987, we would be in Belgrade, Yugoslavia, learning about this part of the world and meeting and talking with university students. He had been there before and knew people who were involved in this program. I paid the $1,200 and then signed up for a passport at the post office. Anytime you enroll in a school, you must have the necessary documents, the right papers. Someone has to agree to these papers and that you have a right to be there. Bills are paid and the school is ready for you. Similarly, when you travel, you also must have some papers, some identification, and plans. Most important is the passport, always keep it in a safe place. If it is ever lost, you must go to the nearest consulate of your country or embassy.

About a week before we left, I had decided I better learn something about this Yugoslavia, so I read some brochures and *World Book Encyclopedia*. I realized through this information that Yugoslavia was a loosely formed country after World War I. The "powers that be" were hoping that this warring area would finally cooperate if they were put together. Eventually, it was time to pack for Yugoslavia. Finally, we went, about twelve of us, from Atlanta to Frankfurt, and then a flight to Belgrade, Yugoslavia. Today, Yugoslavia has vanished into history, and now Belgrade is the capital of Serbia. Essentially, the idea of Yugoslavia did not work out, and each country broke away and regained its independence. The war in this area started (supposedly) when the controlling country, Serbia, tried to keep the countries aligned with them. Each of these countries has its own enigmatic version of this and how it impacted them.

Frankfurt, Germany, was a fun, modern city, and there were some nice historic old parts, but the worst part of this trip was the snoring from a roommate! (A completely different but important topic—travel and sleep.) Frankfurt was like some busy American city with lots of modern shiny buildings, just with a different language. There are some interesting old, preserved parts of Frankfurt, but most of the area was heavily bombed in World War II. This was my first experience being in another country. Although we were only there overnight, I could tell this place was very, very different. Smells, language, currency, and food are some of the more impactful impressions. But we were headed to another place even farther away, and Germany was just a quick stop.

The trip to Belgrade took place two days later. Everything changed even more—different smells, buildings, people's faces. I will never forget the aroma of cigarettes in that hotel. I was awakened early every morning by the smell of cigarette smoke in the restaurant or lobby area. We learned about the city and the country and met some students who had gotten involved with our program. We even took a forty-minute "fun" flight to Dubrovnik (on something like "Yugoair") for twelve dollars round trip! Dubrovnik in 1987 was a shock compared to the cloudy gray city of Belgrade. Rugged limestone against a bright turquoise Adriatic Sea created a beautiful contrast. People wearing native clothes—handmade heirlooms of white, black, and red, tassels, and unique hats pointed in various ways—combined to contrast against our modern polyester travel clothes. The most impressive part was the ancient city-state of Dubrovnik created out of stones and encircled by an imposing wall of rock. I had never seen anything like this.

All of it intrigued me, but still I was firmly planted on USA soil. The world and all of its interesting ports and famous sites were too far away, too remote and unfamiliar. I kept the brochures and various programs of some of the cultural activities, and I wrote to some of the people I met. The experience in Dubrovnik was a highlight. An ancient town of stone, built near the Adriatic Sea. Whereas, the capital of Yugoslavia, Belgrade, was a dirty city, still impacted by bombs from World War II. And the idea of a socialist land of the South Slavs seemed overall a misfit; this notion of Yugoslavia did not seem to be working out. It was held together by Tito's ideas and the police; it was a soft version of communism. Basically in a simple explanation, this part of the world was forced to come together, six countries, and become the "land of the South Slavs"—thus, Yugoslavia. Tito tried to lessen the nationalistic sympathies of each country and to get these former enemies to unite. And for a while it worked, with inter-marriages, people moving to different parts of Yugoslavia, singing songs, and learning Serbo-Croatian. Yet underneath was always the strong tide of each individual country. On Sunday evenings in the large city park, people from Belgrade would gather. Some of our group went there, and I could sense something was not right, or something was going on. Many people were dressed in native clothes and were gathered together singing sad and woeful songs, with such fervent attitude and passion. Overall, for me it seemed to make life complicated, this world vision or idea, the culture, language, customs, travel, time—it's too complex, let's just focus on the USA and get back home. (Soon after this trip, Yugoslavia went into a war.)

Like many people from large countries, I was quite content where I was. I needed to be pushed, prodded, and cajoled into traveling to another country. And, when I did get the passport and traveled to Yugoslavia, I was very intrigued and entertained, and it expanded my ideas and worldview. I heard new languages, experienced different tastes, saw how people looked differently, and stepped out of my comfort zone, and it was almost like entering a dynamic university. A school based on personal experience where the lesson is how the world works. But when I got home, I basically shoved it all into a closet and closed the door.

One difference I could tell was that if I met someone from Yugoslavia, it was great! It was fun to hear about their own story within Yugoslavia and to share about my trip. They could not believe that I had been there. And, the second change, if I heard something on the news about Yugoslavia, or something on the weather, I was intensely interested.

Zvonimir

January of 1994. I met this young man, Zvonimir, eating at the student cafeteria. What a name; I loved the pronunciation. He told me he was from Bosnia and Herzegovina, but a Croatian, and I thought, *I have no idea what he is talking about.* We talked during the meal and afterward he invited me to his room for a coffee. He prepared for me a Turkish-style coffee—most of the coffee grounds settle in the bottom of the cup. It was a gesture of Bosnian kindness to a stranger. Every time I saw him, I knew he would invite me to his room for a coffee. We got to know each other. He was older than the typical student because he had been fighting in the war, and I could tell something was not right. He told me he had post-traumatic stress disorder and was taking medication.

Despite all of this, he was a sweet, kind man, and we enjoyed talking. One day I went to visit him and he was not there. A roommate told me where he was and I wanted to visit him. He was staying in a sanatorium for soldiers. I was determined to find him and see how he was. I found out the address and eventually found the location; when I saw him, I could tell he was not well.

Several months later, during the summer when he was home in Sarajevo, I was also there, and I went to visit him. His family lived in a building with many flats, and his mother had prepared some food for my arrival. I stayed there with him for a few days in the most humble of situations. It was very hot and there was no air-conditioning. We went to a soccer match, and one day it was so hot, so I told him to get his bathing suit. I asked the main hotel if I could pay for us to use the swimming pool, which made Zvonimir very happy.

He was representative of many young men across Yugoslavia who became entrapped in the horrors of the Yugoslav Wars. I lost contact with him, but I pray, Zvonimir, that you are okay, and I thank you for all the coffee you made for me and how kind and special you made me feel, as a stranger in your country.

P. S. Note to travelers: I encourage folks to write in a journal. Just put down the date, where you are, and what happened that day. Something I enjoyed was to choose one postcard each day to put inside. And, if you are willing to learn more, and go to school, then answer these questions: What did you learn about yourself? What did you learn about home? What did you learn about the globe—the culture and the geography of the world?

Chapter Six:

Good and Bad Tourism

S cenario. Fall of 1993. When you live in central Europe, trains are a normal way of travel. The first year in Zagreb, we lived a ten-minute walk from the main train station. When you are on a trip with others, it is continuously entertaining. If you are traveling alone, you are often sitting in one of the "cabins" with others you don't know. Usually, the cabin will have three on one side, or four, and the same on the other. It is a fairly close situation. Occasional glances at the people across from you result in some uncomfortable situations, and they quickly look away because they were also looking at you. Before departure, outside the window, the family members of the passengers would gather. Hands on windows, constantly saying, "Bok, Bok, Bok" (local for hello or good-bye—meaning greeting with God), each person looking with a variety of expressions. This would go on until we departed. Departures during travel can remind one of the fragile nature of our relationships. Train travel is so convenient, so relaxing, that I wonder what happened in the American mindset to let it go and replace it with cars.

Train travel brings people together, even strangers. You are free to relax, have a picnic, read, work on your computer, or call folks you need to talk with. Some trains even offer "quiet cars" where no phone calls are allowed. Children love it and are thrilled about the train experience. You don't have to worry about parking; the train always goes to the center of the city.

With car travel, you don't have to worry about anyone else except you or your family. You can listen to what you want, drive the way you want, and have the temperature set in exactly the way you want. But you have to focus on the road because you are driving.

There are different classes at the "school of travel." These include the cultures of Germany, Netherlands, Belgium, France, Spain, Switzerland, and more. In addition, you will learn about geography, language, travel, and knowledge of current affairs in these countries.

A Lifetime of Travel

This is a brief overview of where I was living and working while in central Europe if you're interested in knowing the actual chronology and locations of where I've lived. This sets a foundation for the rest of the book.

1987: Ten-day work trip to Belgrade, Yugoslavia.

1990: Two-month work program in Belgrade, Yugoslavia.

1992: Two-month work program in Bucharest, Romania, followed by a two-week trip through central Europe, mainly Germany (Bavaria).

1993–1994: Sixteen-month work program in Zagreb, Croatia, including six weeks in Israel.

1995 (March): Ten-day work visit in Zagreb, Croatia.

1996–1997: Sixteen-month work program in Zagreb, Croatia, including six weeks in Israel.

(After this time, I switched careers from Cru to academics.)

1998–2003: I spent almost six years at the University of Georgia, USA, and obtained several degrees.

1998: Two-month travel in Croatia and Europe.

2000: Two-month travel in Croatia and western Europe.

2002: Two-month travel in Croatia and western Europe.

2004–2007: Work in Zagreb, Croatia, as an independent researcher and guest lecturer at the University of Zagreb, and assistance with Udruga Fokus (Croatian name for Cru).

2007–2019: Associate Professor in Olomouc, Czech Republic, Palacký University, Faculty of Physical Culture (Sport and Physical Education).

During this time, it should be noted that I returned to the USA usually twice a year. During these trips, I would often stay in some European city during this transportation. And sometimes, I would travel through Europe at the beginning or the end of this time to several countries for brief tourist visits. This allowed for some extensive travel throughout central and western Europe exposing me to the variety of issues in travel. For example, in 1994 after the fourteen months in Zagreb, Croatia, I had decided, instead of flying to the USA directly, I would meander through Europe and go all the way to London and fly home from there.

Good Tourism/Bad Tourism

Because I was exposed to so much tourism and travel, I began to see travelers who were "behaving" and others who were not. Eventually, I began to develop an ethic of travel, which I want to share with you, the traveler. Some folks call this "sustainable tourism" or "ethical travel." As a child, you were taught the "golden rule" of how to treat others. It goes a long way in many of life's situations. "Do unto others (while traveling), as you would have them to do (while traveling) unto you." Here are a few suggestions:

Keep clean. Put trash away, and pick up trash you see. Protect and guard the environment where you are traveling. Like a child who goes to visit a friend, be on your best behavior. Try to fit in with dress, learn some of their language, speak quietly, and do not be demanding. Look for the authentic. Don't eat McDonald's in Paris or buy T-shirts made in China in Prague. Look for the real aspect of where you are traveling and support that. For example, avoid Disneyland in Paris, but go to Disneyland in California. Ask locals where you can eat local food. Avoid souvenirs or souvenir shops. Look for and support local culture and art.

Meet a local. If you do not meet a local, then you have not really been there! Support the local community rather than large industrial travel companies that are located elsewhere. Treat others the way you want to be treated. Stay at least two nights in one place, and maybe more. Pay everything that is required of you—public transport before you get on the vehicle, tips if required—and always bring a host a small gift (flowers are always welcome).

Those of you interested in this subject can find a lot of information on the internet under these words: responsible travel, eco-friendly travel, sustainable travel, overtourism.

Chapter Seven:

Trains, Trains, Trains

S cenario. In 1994 in Zagreb, the city was full of refugees from the Yugoslav Wars. We were talking and meeting with students. One student wanted to take us to a special café where his friends were. We eventually arrived, after walking through the cold streets of Zagreb. The winter chill was settling on the city, and light fog was giving the old town an eerie effect. There was hardly anywhere to sit, and we had to look hard for a place and crowd in with others. Someone was singing a woeful song. I could hardly see the ceiling, there was so much cigarette smoke. Soon lights filled the room from cigarette lighters. In this crowded café in Zagreb where Bosnian students gathered, their small flame from cigarette lighters, being waved back and forth, seemed to give everyone a sense of togetherness and hope. On the way home, my Yugoslav friend said, "Donald, we are very sad. We are all Bosnian. Most of our land is occupied now. We are sad for that."

Learning the Globe–the Culture and Geography of the World

Trips and excursions may evolve from pleasure retreats to specific learning ventures. Rather than just a quick three-week tour through Italy, the traveler returns with specific knowledge about the culture and geography of Italy. These sojourners have seemingly metamorphosed into colonies of workers who are unearthing the terra firma by discovering and learning its culture and geography.

Learning about Home

One of the aspects of learning is that which involves learning about home. Rediscovering one's dwelling in a faraway land creates a new perspective about home. This type of learning is usually set within a series of contrasts, realizing what is different between home and the places one visits. Interestingly, travelers return with a dual knowledge, a greater appreciation of home as well as a more discerning perspective.

A common theme is that travelers return with a stronger, more positive appreciation of home. This new perspective of home could be a desire to return to that which is most culturally comfortable. Yet the context is that after traveling there is a longing to return to home and a greater appreciation about home.

Trains

Europe is full of trains. They go almost everywhere, and if one track ends, the traveler can catch a bus to go to even the most remote hamlet. However, reading the train information and understanding it in another language can be another ordeal. Sometimes I was shocked at the number of people on the trains. On many trips, there would not even be a place to sit or to stand, and there would be people sitting on the floors. This was often on Fridays or Sundays. One of the biggest surprises when I first went to Croatia was the crowded trams in the city and the crowded trains, especially on weekends. This was mainly because of so many students not having cars as well as the people are used to using the public transport.

And in busy train stations, they often do not give out the information about your train until the train arrives. There will be a crowd of people with eyes firmly fixed on some electric board, and then when some information is put there, there will be a rush to the train. I would find someone who speaks English and ask them to help me understand. The tickets are given with a time, a platform, and a place to be when the train comes. Written in a different language, it can be hard to understand.

The train is connected by "cars" with open seating, and there are cars with an enclosed sitting area for about six to eight people. Inside the enclosed booth, everyone becomes a newly formed group—glancing at one another and the things each have brought. I have been in friendly nice ones, and then in some where no one spoke at all. Sometimes I would say, "Does anyone speak English?" and if so, it could lead to a great conversation on many topics. If no one did, everyone looked away.

Most of my travel experiences on the train were enjoyable, fun, and very relaxing. Leaving all the issues of driving to another person, I could sit and immerse myself in a book, or research, or journal while interesting sights were outside the window and constantly changing. And almost like stepping back in time, sometimes there was a "dining car" with tables, where you could order food or drinks, or just sit and have a coffee. It was a lot of fun to go to the dining car and have a coffee and just sit and look or read. (I would feel like I was in some movie, sitting in a dining car, sipping on a cappuccino, with the beautiful nature passing by, and interesting folks walking through the train.) Of course, not all trains have these dining cars.

One of my favorite train rides was from Zagreb, Croatia, to Salzburg, Austria. You could drive this in five or six hours, but on the train, it's a longer journey from 7:30 a.m. to about 6 p.m. But the view, the scenery, is amazing. You leave the city of Zagreb, and in about three hours, begin to ascend the Alps with all its accompanying views, small churches, villages neatly organized, walking paths, local people, waterfalls, rivers, and high soaring peaks with snow and glaciers, and then you come down on the other side and land in the amazing town of *The Sound of Music*—Salzburg. It's a great train ride, and I highly recommend it.

Here is a creative alpine hut, somewhat typical of what one will find all over the Alps. This was located in Berchtesgaden National Park, Germany.

Scenario. Summer of 1996. I had been on a trip in western Europe and was trying to get from Nice, France, to Grenoble, France. I had read that if you must take this train at night, to be especially careful. This trip was known for thieves who were cleverly getting on the train and getting off at the next stop before anyone could stop them. I got on board, and I saw a man chaining his suitcase with a large metal chain to a post in the middle of the train car! It was like we were preparing for some war. I met a man in the French military and we talked, but we were sitting in different places. I had sort of spread out in one of those enclosed rooms on the train. The train did stop at one station, and I could tell some people were getting on. These folks were walking through the train and looking at everyone, and I was thinking, *Okay, this is it.* Then one young boy came into my compartment, he looked at my watch (an old Timex Ironman watch) and said in broken English, "You have really nice watch." I thought, *How strange, what is going to happen next? This is the train ride from hell!* So I grabbed all my stuff, everything I could gather, and got out of that compartment and went to find the man I talked to earlier, who was in the military, and sat next to him. I was surprised there were no police or train officials anywhere around. We all survived, and it added to an interesting travel experience.

In my research, many travelers stated how they were learning about specific topics of history, various cultures, languages, life in different countries, and the differences between popular cities. And often the guidebook had become a personal textbook utilized in the context of experiential tourism education. The tourism experience had morphed into a personal class of learning. And there is value in having a handheld book or information on a mobile phone that adds more specific information that matches the immediate need of the tourist. I found that tourists would become self-directed, self-modeled learners by underlining, highlighting, or imagining various trips while studying their own guidebook. This type of learning results in individual efficacy as they understand how to wander and meander among previously unknown and strange places.

Tourism has become its own type of school. However, unlike most schools, once you pay the "tuition" you are free to take any class you desire. This school offers a variety of classes about all topics, specific cultures, languages, and geography, and its textbook is the personal tourism guidebook. Further, this textbook becomes a personal souvenir, even a prized possession, which the participants continue to read and use as a reference in the future. It is a common sight to see a tourist with a guidebook in their hand or a mobile device with all of the information they need.

Chapter Eight:

Yugoslavia and Belgrade

S cenario. Fall of 1993. To sit in a café and have a coffee is a way of life for folks in Zagreb. Hey, I can drink coffee; bring me those big cups of coffee with free refills, and I can do coffee all morning. I used to spend hours in a nearby McDonald's in the USA, working, writing, and drinking their free refilled coffee. But, in Zagreb, the coffee culture has a different way. The coffee, or something like espresso, is in a small cup. It is a very strong coffee, and "cream" for coffee can be hot or cold served from another container. It's all a big production, with lots of noise, fanfare, sitting, and servers. I am thinking, *What will I do? I have drunk this tiny cup of coffee in about ninety seconds and I am looking for a refill.* The person with me is pensive and quiet, looking around and completely at peace, and worse, has not even touched their coffee. I had to learn that going for coffee is an art in this area. It's recess, it's getting away, and it's relaxing. I learned not to touch my coffee unless the Croatian I was with had touched theirs. I would make it last with a glass of water for thirty minutes, then I would order another. I was amazed that if I wanted to meet with someone, all I had to say was, "Would you like to go for a coffee?" Almost like magic, they would stop what they are doing and join me in this national pastime. I learned to drink coffee with milk, and also order a coke, or a chocolate, or a Cedevito. It was there at the corner café that the issues of life were solved and sorted into their appropriate categories.

The school of travel offers a special class on the country of Yugoslavia, and the city of Belgrade, its capital. Students will learn about the city, including language, customs, history, and make new playmates (locals) during recess.

Lessons Learned while Working in Belgrade, Yugoslavia, in the Summer of 1990

I learned a lot from my seven-week stay in Belgrade during the summer of 1990, and I want to share some of those lessons with you now.

God loves everyone; not just Americans, but also people called Yugoslavs. Yugoslavia was created after World War I, perhaps in hopes that by putting these nearby countries together they would get along. Yugoslavia had almost twenty-three million people, divided among six states—this included Montenegro, Macedonia, Croatia, Serbia, Bosnia and Herzegovina, and Slovenia. They are a very proud people, proud of their past and culture, but there are a lot of bitter war experiences in this area. Among the faiths, you will find Orthodox people, Catholics, and Muslims; however, these expressions of religion are often cultural. For example, if you are Slovene, you are Catholic. If you are Montenegrin, you are Orthodox. And if you are Bosnian, you are Muslim. Yet I met Catholics, Muslims, and Orthodox people in each of these six countries, and interestingly, there were a lot of atheists. Further, some of the smaller denominations, like Baptists or Jehovah's Witnesses or Mormons, were considered "sect" or strange. I did it all. I was in Catholic Mass, even going to Medjugorje; I got on my knees with worshippers at a mosque in Sarajevo and washed my dirty hands outside; and I stood in many Orthodox churches considering their medieval paintings and lack of pews.

Religious statues on the walk to the Svatý Kopeček church near Olomouc, Czech Republic. One can walk past the fourteen stations of the cross on the way to the church.

Scenario. I met one young man playing basketball—Koki. These big Serbian fellows loved to play basketball. We would walk onto the court, and they would be taking off their pants and playing in their underwear! (Quite simple, no need for extra clothes, a shower, or a changing room). And, if I played, they could talk about playing basketball with an American. We played several Saturdays, and after wiping away sweat and putting on their pants, they invited me to join them for "burek" (sort of a roll stuffed with hard cheese or spinach or sausage) and yogurt that you shake.

Later, they invited me to join them one Saturday night; we went to Koki's friend's place, and everyone was smoking cigarettes and watching MTV. I did not smoke and rarely watched MTV. His friend lived with his family in this huge building, called the Eastern City Gate of Belgrade. Hard to believe that even though we were in a typical flat, it was the entire space for a four-person family. They were all medical students, and somehow, we were discussing evolution, and I mentioned I did not believe in it. They were shocked, and I explained it does not work with the second law of thermodynamics. They were surprised and said that this was the first time anyone had ever given them a cause to doubt this. I knew they were all smart and potentially important for the future of their country. I was happy to try to push their views to be more open to thoughts of God.

Koki and me back in 1990 at his parents' flat in Belgrade.

Furthermore, most of the people there are traditionally Christian Orthodox, concerning their religion. I did not know what it meant to be "Orthodox." I thought it was someone who was really strict, or who followed rules, but we were told that the Serbs are Christian Orthodox in their faith. So, I went to the largest (still in construction) Orthodox church in Serbia, located in Belgrade. Huge building. I eventually went to many Serbian Orthodox churches. To an outsider, they are very similar to Catholics, with some notable differences. Each country has its own order, or pope. That is why there are Greek Orthodox, Serbian Orthodox, and Russian Orthodox. Also, the priests can marry. Within the church, often there are no pews, and people stand for the service. And there is a gate across the front of the altar. I enjoyed the medieval paintings on the walls and the artwork inside the churches. It's very interesting to go to a religious service in another language. My thoughts were often of the uniqueness of language and all of the various languages that were praying to God. Also their pictures or paintings of God or Jesus were medieval, rather than the happy and smiley Western views. When you go to Catholic or Orthodox churches, one can sense the long history of the churches, their complicated past, and realize what a radical Martin Luther was for breaking away and creating something called "protest-ant."

It's hard when you're a stranger. If you are a stranger, or unknown, people there ignore you, look the other way, or sort of push you to the side; there is not a sense of friendliness toward people they don't know. Of course, being a Southerner, living in the charm of Southern hospitality, and growing up in a small town made me more sensitive to this issue. Regardless, if someone does not know you, then it's best to keep out of people's way. Despite their rough manner toward strangers, if you get to know them, they are very warm and friendly.

The people knew a lot about the USA. We would often meet students in various ways; the city is full of them. They were usually glad to meet an American and to go for a coffee. I would always be shocked at their knowledge of the USA's policies toward their country. "Donald, we are still frustrated that in 1920 your secretary of state declined to .... and made this action against our country ..." I would simply stare at them with surprise at their knowledge of politics and history. I was trying to meet young college students and share with them some Christian spiritual information, but some of them even twenty years younger than I was knew so much more than I did about history, geography, or world politics.

At the beginning of this summer program, Cru gave us some training on how to meet students as well as how to have a successful summer. Then we took a twelve-hour train ride from the glitz of Vienna to the dirty streets of Belgrade. There was a group of us—we would look for college-age students and approach them and say: "Izvinite . . . do you speak English? I am from the USA, and I am here in your country this summer. May we join you for a few minutes and ask a few questions? What is Yugoslavia like? What are your religious views? If you don't have time now, can we meet later?" Although it was somewhat intrusive and unusual, most everyone, out of hospitality, would stop what they were doing, and usually we would sit in a café and have a coffee. They had a very positive and almost adoring view of the USA. I rationalized that this may have been because of our movies and music, our reputation as the defender of democracy, and the idea that they could go there and make money. And many of them had relatives who had lived and worked in the USA. So they listened to us. By the way, this is a very misunderstood part of mission life: most of the students couldn't care less about what we were saying, as most were atheists. They listened to us only because we were from the USA and speaking understandable English. Many of them were glad to meet an American, and if we met them again, they would often bring a friend who was just as impressed.

The people of Yugoslavia were very educated, spoke English, and really liked the USA. They were living with much less materially than what we were used to. Most Americans are unaware of their wealth and surplus compared to others. I was surprised at their interest in meeting an American and talking with us. We met many young Serbian college students who were passionate about their country and "Greater Serbia." I had no idea what they were talking about. They knew more about my history than I did, and they were very curious and passionate about discussing politics. We would try to listen to them and share information about the Bible, but they seemed to think they already knew all of that.

You can buy beautifully crafted items there. I would see older ladies sitting in parks, working on some needlework. They knew that tourists were in this area, and I could not resist them. I bought several items such as handmade or embroidered fabrics (some people call them "doilies"), which I still have. These sweet women were just sitting there in the park and sewing some beautiful handiwork. They were authentic Serbian ladies doing something with their hands, creatively trying to make some extra money. I also bought some crystal vases made in Yugoslavia. The prices of these vases and their beauty made them very attractive.

The people didn't have much money, but they were happy. Yugoslavian folks are well educated, and the school system through high school has a high academic value. Most everyone who attends the university speaks two or three languages well. There weren't many cars, maybe one per family, and there were no parking places; people parked everywhere, especially on sidewalks. And there were no dryers for clothes. It seemed to me the country was in an economic disarray. For example, folks lived in these "flats," which were usually in large buildings with up to a thousand residents. People who lived in the cities were often in large buildings that were built by the company they worked for. A typical family of four would have two or three rooms, and sitting rooms would often double as bedrooms. The people seem to be physically big. Have you seen the Serbian basketball team or the Croatian water polo team? It was hard for me to reconcile that although they lived with so little, they were so smart, happy, and funny. During this time, 1992, there were no drying machines, garbage disposals, or ice makers in homes there. I realized how much simpler life was without these, and also wondered whether they were really necessary. Another interesting aspect of life is that I do not recall anyone calling themselves a Yugoslav. Each of them labeled themselves by what country they were actually from.

You have to pay to use the public toilets. Belgrade is a densely populated city around one million, with a huge population of college students. Most of the talented students end up in Belgrade. We would meet students in various places in the town. This called for the use of public toilets, which became its own interesting experience. You had to pay for the toilet and extra for the toilet paper. There were public toilets around with someone working in them, and paying for it seemed so odd. And then if you did not pay for extra toilet paper and brought it with you, you might be in trouble.

People are the same everywhere. Although we were on a mission, we were having a lot of fun. It was very easy to meet students—they are friendly anyway—and we would invite them for a coffee, and they loved to sit in cafés and drink coffee. Underneath these obvious differences, we could see that people basically are the same as us. Families, work, school—people fall in love, marry, work, and have their own children. Grandparents are close by and are involved with the family. People love to laugh and enjoy life and relax. People want a government they can trust that will take care of their civil needs. One obvious distinction for me was that I could see how much easier life is in the USA with 335 million people, with one language, one currency, and an easy way to move around (roads and cars). We have had only one major war on our land and that was a civil war, not an invading army.

McDonald's tastes the same everywhere. Sometimes we would get homesick and start thinking about US food. But, guess what, they had McDonald's! Nothing like the one you see in your hometown, this one had chandeliers, nice chairs, and large cabinets, and it was almost like a living room. But the food was the same, and it tasted just like it does in the USA. And the crowd! I had never seen such a crowded McDonald's.

Also complicating my getting some American food was this line of people that made no sense. I was used to a very straight line that went back from the cash register. (Later I understood that this is also a very Western idea.) This was a large mob of people that sort of moved in a random way, front, back, left, and right. And, if someone walked in, and they saw someone they knew in the line, it was considered okay to break the line to join them. But eventually, we did get our taste of American food. When we ordered the food, in our native English, the looks and stares we received were interesting. I could see they were giving me a place and respect that I did not deserve.

The food is nice. We were living in Belgrade, the capital of Yugoslavia, for almost seven weeks. I was with a group of students from the USA, a group of four men and four women. We lived in separate homes. We would meet students during the day, and at night, we would all go out for dinner together and eat in restaurants. Some great food we had in Belgrade! Šopska salad (pronounced shopska with a long o), all sorts of meat cooked on the grill, salads, and lots of potatoes.

Yugoslavia was literally falling apart, and we did not even know it. I saw many people dressed in old native clothes, singing songs of which I knew nothing. Now I realize they were extremely patriotic and singing of the old days and wars of Serbia. Within a year, Croatia, Slovenia, Macedonia, and Bosnia and Herzegovina had separated from Yugoslavia, leaving just Serbia and Montenegro. Serbia went to war with the other countries to try to retain them inside Yugoslavia. Today, they have returned to their pre–World War I status, of separate countries with their own flags, languages, and capitals.

Nudity is normal. The Danube River flows right through the middle of Belgrade. And within this river is an island called Ada Ciganlija. Here are all types of recreation, including basketball courts, places for swimming, "fudbal" fields, and some trails through woods. We would often go there and enjoy this urban area of recreation. In the summer, most men wear small bathing suits and women may be topless. I remember seeing a very large man, sitting down, and it looked as if he was naked because his tiny little bathing suit was covered over by his body. He was not self-conscious, just proud to be there, absorbing the sun. You could see other people standing and facing the sun in their various positions, giving their body full exposure to the sun. And, as in every place in this part of Europe, there was an area for nude swimming and sunbathing.

Overall, this two-month stint in Belgrade was really my first true experience abroad. I should add that I almost backed out of this trip; my dad died two months before I was supposed to go. As with most reluctant travelers, the push I needed to continue came through the realization that he had traveled a lot during his tenure in the Navy during World War II, as well as the realization that what else could be done for him? It impacted me living in another country for this long period (two months). We were doing some tourist activities, but really we were living in their neighborhoods, meeting and talking with people, mainly students, and we were able to learn more about their lives. I could see the difference between being a tourist and living there. I realized that rather than being a tourist, staying for two or three days, I preferred staying longer, and I was hoping that someday I could live there for a longer time.

Chapter Nine:

Romania and Bucharest

cenario. Fall of 2007. I am inside the toilet, or water closet. It is a single tiny room, with only space for a commode. And that is it; there's nothing else in this room. In order to wash my hands, I have to cross the hallway and go into the bathroom, which has a sink, bathtub, and washing machine. I have to wait to wash my hands because the washing machine is now emptying into the sink. Above the washing machine is a hot water heater that is turned on twenty minutes before you want a bath, and then it's turned off. Above the sink is a drying line with towels and a few clothes (there are no dryers). The kitchen is rather small, but there's enough room to cook adequate meals for this family of five. There is a kitchen table. And if there are more than five, you take turns sitting and eating. There are three additional rooms; two are bedrooms, and one is a sitting room with a television.

All three children share one bedroom, and the parents are in the other. Outside the sitting room is a "working patio" where one does chores. This is where clothes dry, and there are some potted plants and various mops. After dinner, we all go down the stairs, speaking to other neighbors who live in the building as we pass, and outside for a walk in the outdoors. This is a typical home/flat in central Europe, and they are completely adequate and functional. The building is surrounded by a grassy area, which is taken care of by the city. The residents meet monthly and organize themselves for necessary civic responsibility, such as keeping snow off the sidewalk. Each person in the building has a basement room for storage about the size of a large closet. This is the usual place where winter or summer tires are stored. Once a month, a group of workers will show up and clean or do what is necessary outside in the yard, or grass, or garden area. Around the building are some strange-looking iron structures. Finally, someone explains what they are to me. They're left over from years ago, when there were no vacuum cleaners, so people would bring their rugs down here and beat them to get the dirt out. There was a special wooden object for this "beating" or cleaning of the rugs.

Silvije

I met Silvije in the fall of 1993, a referral from a previous Christian program. He was a veterinary student, very friendly, and he had a lot of friends whom he wanted me to meet. I would meet him once a week, and we would talk and read the Bible together. He taught me a lot about Croatian and Slavonian life, people who live east of Zagreb. "Donald, come in. I am very hungry; I am going to make our version of your 'peanut butter and jelly' sandwich," he says, laughing, and he opens a closet door, changes his clothes into something more comfortable, and then carefully peels a clove of raw garlic, and after spreading it on bread, he hungrily takes a bite. "This is so nice and tasty!" As the aroma of garlic fills the room, we open the Bible and read.

Later in the year, I went to visit Silvije at his family home near Nova Gradiška. His parents were so nice and welcoming to me. Like many Croatians, they have a flat in a building near their work, and they are saving money and will start to organize the building of a separate home, usually on some family property. They will never borrow money for this, but save it, and then they will build when they get money, floor by floor, first the foundation, maybe the basement, then the next year, the second floor, and then later the third; then they will add the kitchen, and then finish the house, and slowly move in—this can take ten to twenty years. Sheet rock is rarely used at all, but rather thick walls of concrete, or brick. And often it is friends and neighbors who help to build, or if there is a need, they will call in experts. Almost all the homes have a red tile roof. Folks there asked me, "Is it true in your country that you have roofs made of paper?"

Eventually they will move in, and then may give the original flat or apartment to one of their children, and another child may move in with their family into this home, but on another floor. Silvije also took me on a ride around the area, which is near the Sava River, a very rural area. We passed many farmers pulling wagons with horses, and we saw many stork nests on poles, a very large bird with a huge nest made of sticks.

Several years later when I returned to Croatia, Silvije was getting married, and he made a special invitation for me to join. One lady in Zagreb said, "Listen, Donny, if you are invited to a wedding in our country, it is a special invite, and especially in this Slavonian area, you must give him at least one hundred dollars or more. You cannot give him some twenty-dollar gift like some Americans would do, and you must be prepared to stay up the entire night." Somewhat nervous, I drove to Gradiška where the wedding was, and I found the home of Silvije. It was about 3 p.m. When I entered the home, the house was full of food, people were mingling around, and there was a group of men in native dress singing. Silvije was in the middle of this. He saw me and welcomed me. We ate some food and listened to the singing, and everyone was making merry. I went for a walk and then returned to change for the wedding. Many of us were going to the wedding by bus. We got to a church and the ceremony began, a traditional Catholic wedding. After the wedding, the entire crowd came up and congratulated the new couple inside the church. The couple stood in front of the altar, and the entire congregation lined up and each person shook hands and hugged and kissed. (I thought, *Well, this must be it. We congratulate them, and then are we leaving?*)

Then we get back on the bus and go to some restaurant. There was a feast of food laid out as well as local specialties made by the families. The wine was from their vineyard, and there were small homemade biscuits. There were speeches, and dances, and many other events, some of which I did not understand. A large dinner was served. The most fun was when everyone was in a circle going round and round; it sounded to me like Gypsy-style music. There was a lot of food, and a lot of wine. This started after the wedding, about 7–8 p.m., and did not stop until Silvije and Ankica left, which was 6 a.m. the next day!!! Almost every two hours, they would bring out more food, and the wine was continuously being refilled. When I got back on the bus, I was sort of just sitting there until someone told me what to do. Silvije's mother said, "Come on," and put me asleep in an empty bed; I think it was 6.30 the next morning! We mostly slept that morning, and after waking, we had some breakfast, and then I left. It was a special experience. Another person told me that is the minimum length of a Slavonian wedding, whereas the more traditional ones can be three days long. I thought no wonder everyone is so tired. It would render you useless to go to one of these; it is like staying up all night. No wonder some people I know refuse to attend weddings there. Silvije and I are still in touch.

Romania

Scenario. June of 1992. The streets of Bucharest were kept clean by Roma folks sweeping them with large brooms; the brooms looked homemade and were created out of reeds or sticks! Occasionally in this large European capital, you would see a mule-drawn cart going down the road hauling trash or wood. In 1992, the Romanians were climbing out of the hole left by a difficult communist dictator and regime. Just behind the building where we were staying, there was a large pile of trash that could cover two football fields. I can remember walking in this area and children were playing their own version of soccer with a homemade "ball" made out of trash. They were having a game, laughing and enjoying themselves. I thought about how simple life can be, that in a field surrounded by trash, in a country that had collapsed, children were laughing, playing their own version of soccer with a ball made from trash. I also thought about how different life is in the USA, not having to deal with forty years of communism.

We had never seen such poverty—
a young woman pushing a cart with a broom made of sticks.

With the same organization (Campus Crusade for Christ, International—now Cru), we were supposed to return to Yugoslavia to continue the work we were doing with students. Eventually, we were told that Yugoslavia was now at war, falling apart, and was not safe. We were asked if we would be interested in joining another group that was going to Romania. So, in the summer of 1992, a small group of us headed to Bucharest instead of Belgrade.

Bucharest, Romania

Similar to before, we had some training, and then we flew into Bucharest. In 1992, it was like a ghost town—smoke rising from fires in trash cans, complete darkness at night due to a lack of streetlights, and hardly anyone moving around the town. This was a dense urban area, with a lot of buildings, but everything seemed empty. Strangely, they took us to a Chinese restaurant for dinner. As if we were not having enough cultural shock, we were now going to eat Chinese food in Romania. We moved into our places for sleeping, and we were scattered all over the town of Bucharest. Because it was a change of plans, we really did not know anything about this place. We began to learn more and meet the local people who also worked with this group, including some Americans and many Romanians.

We learned that there was a very strict communist rule here for around forty years. After the fall of communism, their world had changed overnight. Before they would be put into jail for talking to someone from the West, especially an American, and now we were walking down the streets and saying hello. In the middle of Bucharest, there was this outstanding building, built by the dictator Ceaușescu. This beautiful marble building is huge! It was closed to the public; we could only walk around it. This building became known as the palace building of Ceaușescu. It was the seat of government as well as his home or palace. Supposedly, he tore down many neighborhoods to build it. He was known to be a ruthless dictator, imposing his will on the people, and this was one example of that. However, the structure that was built is truly impressive, one of the largest government buildings in Europe. It was heavily guarded and fenced off in '92, but when I returned in '97, I finally got a tour of this amazing building. Yet, for the local people, it is a sad reminder of their past regime.

The man who rented us his flat, Vasili, was so sweet and kind. Four of us shared this large flat, and his wife washed our clothes; they were happy to get some extra money. Every day, we would eat lunch at the Bucharest Hotel, one of the nicest restaurants in town. There were no tourists, there was nothing to see, there were no lights at night, the city was still in lockdown, and acres of trash were everywhere. It was obvious the country was in recovery from the previous regime, and they were learning how to live in this new world.

It was almost like being in some surreal dream for us. Every day we would go to the university to meet students and to talk with them. First, we had to find students who could speak English, or we would take a Romanian with us who could translate for us. We would walk into a dormitory, where the halls were lined with small pots of boiling potatoes and rows of shoes next to their doors. Some students had so little money they could not afford to even eat in the student cafeteria, so they were boiling potatoes for their daily food. Shoes lining the hallways is the traditional way that people who live in central Europe handle shoes. You do not wear outside shoes inside. Four years before, anyone caught talking to us would have been arrested, and now we were knocking on their doors, smiling, and asking them whether we could talk with them. We were trying to share the good news of the gospel, but most of them were more shocked that there was an American at their door. Out of sheer politeness, they would always invite us in and offer us tea or coffee, and they would listen. We tried to show them we cared and that we were interested in them. The hallways and dormitories were easily accessible, so we would just walk into the dorm, knock on a door, and ask them whether they spoke English. If not, we had an interpreter with us. "Hello, hello, my name is Donald, and my friend here is Valitino. We are traveling in Romania for a few weeks and are interested in Romanian students and their views. Maybe we can get your opinion?" Shocked that a Westerner was interested in their views, with wide eyes, they cautiously let us into their room. We would ask a few questions about their views and philosophy of life, including their view of God. We would give them a Christian periodical to read if they were interested. We would all meet up at around 4 p.m. and return to our flats together, and when we would walk to the taxi, it was like there was an American parade on the agricultural campus of the University of Bucharest.

Bucharest, the capital of Romania, is a large European city with a significant cultural heritage all of its own. There is a beautiful opera house, and I noticed something was going on there, so I bought tickets for everyone in our group. Of course, there was no air-conditioning, so it was hot. It was the opera *Madama Butterfly*. I thought, *This is just too ironic*; here we are, a group of Protestant Christian white Americans, sitting in Bucharest, watching an opera about an American soldier in a war in Japan, falling in love with a Japanese woman, and of course, the language was in Italian—quite the cultural concoction. Also in the center of Bucharest was a very large beautiful park, and then outside near the college was a traditional museum with authentic native houses and clothes.

I will never forget the creativity and the sadness (for me) of seeing a real entrepreneur in the middle of the city. He had a bathroom weighing scale, where you step on and see your weight. He was standing in a park, and advertising, "Get your weight for the first time." No one even had the money to have their own bathroom scales, and here was a young man, so desperate that he was creative enough to consider this as a business. I gladly stepped on the scale and paid him about ten cents, and he wrote out my weight in kilograms. He proudly handed me my weight as if he had conducted a significant business transaction.

There was an obvious presence of Roma people in Bucharest, and if the Roma children heard us speaking English, they would run to us with open hands hoping for a few coins or chewing gum. The people I met in Romania who were willing or able to talk to us were some of the kindest, humblest people I have ever known.

After four weeks, we left Bucharest and joined others in our group for a three-week program on the Black Sea. This was very unusual for me, as I had never even heard of the Black Sea. We were in Costinești, a coastal town on the Black Sea. This was a popular vacation area for Romanian people, and within this area, they had special housing for students. We were there to reach the college students. It was hot, but the water was cool. Bathing suits were barely hanging on. It was a student area; they were meant to have fun, and well, you can imagine! We did everything to meet students—walk up to them on the beaches, play volleyball and tug of war, invite them to see a movie about Jesus, and act out dramas in the streets about the popular television show *Dallas* to get them interested in the movie *Jesus*. Showing the ruggedness of the area, they had a waterslide that you would use only once because it was not fitted well, or there were some jagged parts, and you would often end up a little scrapped at the end.

I was always looking out for interesting situations of real Romanian life, and during my time at the Black Sea, I saw a cafeteria with a lot of people going in and out. Our group always ate at a private catered café. But I wanted to try to get more into the Romanian culture, so I went in, and I knew I had entered real Romania. There were no napkins, no salt-shakers. You used the tablecloth for a napkin, and salt and pepper were poured into small bowls, and you used your fingers to pinch together what pepper or salt you wanted. The menu was okay; a lunch was about forty cents for me, but it had everything—some meat, some vegetables, some bread, and a drink. Another time on the Black Sea, farmers were trying to sell their extra produce, and there was a truck with nothing but peaches, as sweet as Georgia peaches, piled high. I saw every sort of bathing suit, as well as anatomy, coming up there and buying peaches from this farmer, including me. There was a special area with an outdoor theater, and we were told there was a nightly comedy, or comedian, there. It was always full, and you could hear the students roaring with laughter.

I will tell you one story about a young man named Daniel, a religious conversion story. His life was frustrating and empty, although he was trying to find meaning through hard rock and academics. One day, an American in our group called Dean knocked at his door and explained to him the gospel. We saw Daniel a few days later, and although he was raggedly dressed, with very long and stringy hair, there was an interest in him and a smile. He explained that he read the gospel of John and had decided to become a follower. "I even got out my matches and burned one of the hard rock posters in my room." We all thought, *Wow, this is great. God bless you.* We explained to Daniel that we were leaving to go to this beach area. We gave him information about folks to contact who could help him with his new faith. When we arrived, Daniel was there waiting for us! Furthermore, he looked completely different! No one even recognized him; he had to motion to us, and come closer. He had cut his hair, simply cleaned up, and he was dressed nicely. It was a shock to see. He said he would be here with us and come to our meetings. It was a unique and rare experience, perhaps only a college student could do it, but it reflected the desperation and focus of the young generation at this time in Romania. Folks like Daniel had lived through the disappointments of communism, as well as the frustration and confusion their new government had brought. We were offering another way, another view of life.

During this time, we took a weekend trip to the mountains of the area beyond Bucharest—the beautiful Carpathian Mountains, where we saw shepherds, Dracula's castle (later I found out there are lots of castles and places that claim Dracula!), and many interesting mountain areas. One day while walking on the tops of these mountains, we saw large herds of sheep and their shepherds. I am from a rural area, but I had never seen a shepherd who was actually living with the sheep. I introduced myself and gave him something to read. The people of Romania were very different from other people I had met in Europe. Shy and without any resources, they would try their best to help you. My favorite stories there were of Dana and Vali, and how they helped us so much to learn how to relate to the people of Romania. The day we left, there was crying and sad fare-wells to our new friends. Now most have changed—married, children, and grandchildren—but the summer of 1992 will always remain a special event in our lives.

On the sandy shore of the Black Sea, in the town of Costinești, there was a half-sunken ship. It was the summer of 1992, and Natalie Cole had just come out with her Grammy award-winning album *Unforgettable*, and strangely it was often playing, for some reason, over the loudspeakers. I thought how interesting that this woman who has also struggled with life, singing such beautiful music, echoing off the sand of the Black Sea, should be heard by people who also have had such a difficult life. How quickly has this area changed, if the voice of a Western singer would be on the loudspeaker? I also realized that governments change, and some-one may be in charge for fifty or more years, but people are stronger than their governments. People everywhere are interested in knowing others, and they respond to kindness and politeness.

Croatia

Serbia

YUGOSLAVIA

Chapter Ten:

Domogoy, Biljana, and Sandra

They were called Domi and BB, and they had been in love since high school and were enjoying life together. It was the time of Yugoslavia, and they were both from Sisak. Eventually, the political divide separated them because one was Croatian and the other was Serbian. Biljana's parent's home had been "bombed" (someone put some homemade explosives near the house), and her

Yes, here is an early picture of this
Yugoslavian couple in love.

parents had been threatened, probably by someone on the nationalist Croatian side. So, her parents left their home and went to the town of Banja Luka in Bosnia where many Serbian people in this area went. This is maybe sixty miles away. Can you believe that after they left, and locked the door, some Croatian broke into the home and claimed the property?

Biljana, however, was in conflict because she loved Domogoy and wanted to be with him, so she decided to stay in Croatia. They figured out how to make this work, and they lived together and went to the university, hoping all would be okay. However, the war worsened, and the conflict between Serbia and Croatia became more intense. This was especially hard on Biljana because her parents were in the Serbian area of Bosnia, and they wanted her to come home. Eventually, they both became closer to God, they married, and the war seemed to go away, but her parents were still in Banja Luka. Years later, they were eventually able to get the person to move out of the home BB's parents built. Similar situations of confiscated properties happened throughout the former Yugoslavia, and many are still in litigation.

Sandra

Sandra and her family in her village on the edge of Croatia. Most of the houses are crowded around the road, and of course, everyone knows everyone.

Sandra was a schoolmate of Biljana and Domogoy. They had known each other for a long time and had been friends. However, Sandra is from a village farther from Sisak, closer to the border of Bosnia. And interestingly, in this village there were more Serbians than Croatians. Her parents lived in this rural part of former Yugoslavia. Sandra was smart and interested in learning, and she had a grandmother who was very focused on her, and who had almost raised her because her parents were working. The influence of the Baka (grandmother) is very strong in this part of the world, and so Sandra went, like BB and Domi, to the University of Zagreb and studied pharmacy. During her school time, the war broke out, and she eventually became separated from her parents. This tiny little village in the woods near Bosnia also became divided according to nationalist interests, and there was trouble because Sandra's dad was Croatian in this mainly dominant Serbian area. Her parents left this area and became refugees in Serbia. Sandra was torn between countries, ideologies, and all that was going on. Sandra also became a believer and eventually married an American whom she met with this group. It was a difficult and sad time for many families caught in the web of this confusing conflict. Sandra's sweet father died during this time, way before his time. Perhaps this undue stress, moving, and pressure from the Serbian influence added to this early demise. Sadly, this was also reflective of many families across Yugoslavia. Life moved on, and Sandra placed her hopes on a brighter focus in life. Together with Domi and BB, they all helped to start a Christian outreach program that's still active in Croatia. You can meet them if you travel to Croatia.

All of these situations took place many years ago. Domi, BB, and Sandra (and Nolan, her husband) all live in Zagreb today, are married with children, and are enjoying their lives. And there is much more to their story than what I shared; over coffee, they would probably love to talk with you in person.

Chapter Eleven:

Conflict in Travel

S cenario. September of 2010. I was with friends in the mountains of North Moravia. We were staying at their traditional Moravian family home in a beautiful setting around Karlov. Mirek (Jaromir) was going mushrooming, and Mirek's family suggested I join him. In my upbringing, we were taught to avoid or step on or kick away a mushroom. Over here, there is a mushroom culture, where they teach children which ones are okay to eat. So I followed him into the woods, a northern European forest that had been heavily cut and regrown, and on the floor of the forest every once in a while would be a mushroom. In the silence, I could hear my mother's clucking tongue and see her finger wagging back and forth. Mirek showed me which ones were okay. Basically, if it looked okay, it should be good to eat; anything that looked strange or was a strange shape or unusual color—avoid. And most important, turn the mushroom over. If there are "gills" on the mushroom, don't take it; it should be smooth. We crawled, cut, crawled, pushed back bushes, cut—and after a few hours, we returned home exhausted with baskets full of varied mushrooms! Mirek spent the rest of the day "cleaning" the mushrooms and organizing them; they would supply a significant part of their winter soups and meals. Near the cabin, outside, there were almost four tables that were covered with mushrooms. One of my favorite local foods is the forest mushroom and potato soup.

This castle in North Moravia was the site of a feudal kingdom with a vast
amount of land for farming. The interior of the castle is much the same as when
it was built. Today, it is a popular wedding site and tourist destination.

Dealing with Conflict while Traveling

Conflicts at the school of travel may happen with teachers and other students. Interesting and difficult things sometimes happen when you travel.

I was on my way home to the USA. I was on the tram, near the train station, and I had forgotten to "stamp" the ticket when I got on the tram. I was focused on the travel, and all of my luggage. I see the guy coming for me to see whether I have a ticket, and I get up to stamp it. He says, "No, get off the tram!" I get off with all my luggage, and he gives me a ticket for 750 Czech koruna, about thirty-five dollars). I could not believe he would pick on me, a stranger in his country, to do this. I kept the receipt he gave me, and I promised myself that when I returned in three months, I would try to get this money back. I had the ticket in my hand, and I simply got distracted when getting on the tram with luggage to go home. How could I get a refund with the language barrier and the time delay—I would not be back for three months—and how would I go about solving this? So, three months later, I returned to this transport office and explained the situation, and they refunded me the ticket. Lesson: Public transport always requires a ticket, and there are people who may check, yet, if you think someone has made a mistake, don't be afraid to take an interpreter and question the ticket.

Public Transport and Stealing

I had been granted permission to give some lectures to students and teachers at a university in Spain, near Alicante. This was part of the teacher exchange program under the Erasmus program. And, on the way back, my university said I could also attend an education-oriented conference where I gave a lecture. It was an exciting time in Spain, in Alicante, and then in Madrid. I had given lectures with all of their accompanying excitements as well as the pride and bigheadedness that comes with that.

It was the day of my return to Olomouc. I had a large suitcase and was staying on the fourth floor of a hotel with no elevator (not a good idea). I had organized everything the night before and left early enough to ride the subway to the airport. I had carefully put all travel documents and some money in a special document right on the front of the large suitcase—one of those pouches on the outside of the suitcase (also not a good idea).

I was riding on the subway and noticed while I was on one escalator that a group had gone around me, and I thought that it was rather crowded. When I got to the airport and opened my outside pouch to get the documents for travel, I didn't see them. I looked again and slowly went through my suitcase, thinking for sure I was just about to find them. The third time, I began to panic.

I opened the entire suitcase in front of the check-in counter and rumbled through it and realized that they were simply not there. I begged the man to just let me on the plane. The man from the airline smiled and simply said he could not allow me to fly without a passport and plane ticket, although my name was listed there on the page for potential fliers.

The only thing I could imagine was somehow, someway, the packet of documents must have been left in the hotel. I found out there was another flight that day. So I went back to Madrid, in the center, hopefully to find all the things there, and then I planned to take the later flight. I went downstairs to check my large piece of baggage into storage. After I paid the fee, they said they couldn't allow this baggage to stay there because of its size. I was really getting frustrated and angry. I begged them to keep it there so I didn't have to take it with me as I rushed back to the hotel. "Sorry, sir, that is a security risk." I knew that it was not, and I was so frustrated at our world that has become so complicated because of terrorists. So, I had to lug this huge suitcase with me all the way back to the city of Madrid to see whether my documents were there. So reluctantly I did it. I arrived at the hotel and the manager was very concerned and tried to help me. We searched the room and nothing. He said to me that the subway is very dangerous and probably somehow someone was able to unzip the outside pocket of the suitcase and get the pouch without me knowing it. It must have happened when I was on the escalator—when the group of people, dressed in everyday outfits, surrounded me, one of them must have quickly gone through the outside zippers of the suitcase.

The hotel manager gave me a coffee, we sat down, and he said, "You must go to your embassy and get another passport." He was very helpful and wanted to come with me to make sure I got to the embassy. I thought that this man was unusually kind. He said he would go with me and take me to the embassy. We were walking there, and going here and there to all places strange to me, and my mind began to run away with negative thoughts. I started to think, *This man has lured me here to harm me or sell me to some zealots.* (I was out of control.) Finally, we arrived at the embassy. The embassy was very nice, we called my university, and they purchased a ticket for the plane, and the embassy expedited my passport. After retrieving my large bag, I was back on the subway to the airport, on the next flight to Prague. Whew, it was an ordeal.

I am not interested in living in a world with people who steal from you or look for someone to take advantage of. The traveler must learn the importance of flexibility in travel and of keeping calm in situations over which they have no control. You do have control of your thoughts. Traveling will put the traveler in many situations where they are out of control. Therefore, learning to control your thoughts can enable you to be calm and more relaxed in these potential situations. Something that has helped me is to meditate on Psalm 23 while I am traveling. I have seen that if I overreact to some difficult situation, it only makes the other person also overreact and defend their position. Lesson: always keep your passport, and cash, around your neck.

Trouble at the Border

In May of 2017, I had been given money from the university to travel to Opatija, Croatia, to attend a conference and make a presentation. And, afterward, I was going to spend some time with friends in Zagreb. During this era, things had changed in the European Union, and Croatia was now part of the European Union. I felt relieved, thinking I could travel more easily and not even need my passport (bad mistake). I traveled with my Czech identity and work card.

I had driven, almost seven hours, all the way from Olomouc, Czech Republic, through complicated Vienna, to the border of Slovenia and Croatia. I was stopped at the border and asked for my passport. I said I had this identity card, not my passport. (My friends were going to meet me for dinner in about two hours, and I was only thirty minutes from Zagreb.) He came back and asked me to park and come inside. He asked me where my passport was, and I said I thought I did not need it, but here is my identity card. He said, "Yes, but you are an American, and you must have a passport." It was getting dark, and he stared at me and said, "You are illegal here and your fine is €400. You are trespassing and must leave within thirty minutes. You must return to the Schengen Area." I begged this man, and he said, "We are having many problems with unauthorized immigrants, and you are not legal without your passport." (€400 was worth about $550.)

I was undergoing huge stress. I wanted so much to attend this conference, and I wanted to see my friends in Zagreb. I could not say or do anything to persuade this man, especially when there were so many unauthorized immigrants around, as they were in a high state of watch. (Even though our first lady at the time was from Slovenia, this did me no good. I called some people and said I did not have the right papers, no passport, and had to return. I paid the man €400 and left. This was a very difficult drive for me in the dark, and on some road under repair, I drove just over the border into the Schengen Area into Austria and stayed at the first hotel I could see. It helped me to keep thinking of positive thoughts, such as quoting from the Bible, John 3:16. I was nervous, scared, angry, and frustrated. The next day I drove back to Olomouc and returned the money to the university. I learned to take care of required documents. And, the sun rose, the day was fine, and all was good in the world. Lesson: anytime you cross an international border you need your passport.

Scary Outdoor "Drama in Real Life"

Once a year, I would attempt to go to the Krkonoše National Park. This interesting national park is on the border of Poland and the Czech Republic. The top of the mountain area is shared by the two countries, both currencies are welcome, and there is a Czech post office and a Polish one. There is also a Czech restaurant and a Polish one. The entire area is a beautiful mountain landscape called the Giant Mountains. Around the base of this area are interesting small villages with trails, ski slopes, spas, and some beautiful vistas. One of my favorite areas is called Modrý důl, a beautiful valley on the Czech side of the mountain and the Una River. On this particular occasion, I had wanted to return to the area called Pec pod Sněžkou, Krkonoše. I had stayed several times at one interesting hotel with a traditional atmosphere called Bouda Máma and wanted to see all of this again. You had to park your car in the village and walk to the hotel; no cars were allowed there.

I had noticed driving into the area that there was already snow on the top of Krkonoše. And worse, I had heard that bad weather was coming. But that day there was a beautiful sunny blue sky, and I thought, *Well, if I have time, maybe I can get up the mountain today.* I saw that the ski lift was working, as before it had been closed for repairs for several years. So I checked into my room, and I thought, *I will go really fast. It's only two miles to the top, and I can catch the newly restored ski lift down.* I took my iPad to take some photos of the sunset, and I wore very little clothes because I knew I would get warm. I brought nothing else with me.

I took off with joy in my heart at the beautiful fall colors and the surrounding areas. The small beginning of the river Una and the nearby valley Modrý důl were all beautiful to see, and I was enjoying my time and looking forward to getting to the top, taking the tram down, and getting dinner at Bouda Máma. We had recently buried my mom, and my thoughts were often on this, handling all the details of her house six thousand miles away, and then the sadness that comes with burying someone you are close to. The walk was a welcome break from university life, and I felt completely at home in this foreign forest because I was outdoors. It was a great chance to pour out my heart and to gain encouragement from God's handiwork.

At the top, the sun was setting and it was a spectacular view. I was able to take several photos. And yes, for sure, there was snow on the top, and it was even deeper than I thought, maybe two to three feet in some places. I had to step in the snow, but I knew I would soon be dry after the short ride down on the gondola. So there I am at the top and it is already dark now, but no worries, because I will take the tram down and be in the hotel in a few minutes. I make my way to the gondola. I do not hear anything, and neither do I see anyone, and then I realize, it has closed. I hit on the shut door to no avail. I am left alone at the top of Krkonoše National Park. These are the highest mountains on the Czech Republic and Poland border. Now it is very dark, it is cold, and the wind is blowing. My heart is racing with anxiety and nervousness. I am thinking, *I cannot die here. I must somehow get somewhere where someone can help me.* I make my way to the Czech post office (on the top of the mountain) and see someone inside; however, he won't open the door. I have only a few Czech dollars, enough for the ride on the gondola, no phone, and no appropriate clothes. I look around and see the Polish motel about three hundred yards away down the mountain. The lights are on and maybe I can get some help there. I chose to think about Psalm 23 and I pray and say this favorite scripture aloud. I talk to God as I am slipping and sliding in the snow in my shorts and in the dark. I know it is too dangerous to try to go down this mountain in this darkness, so I will try to stay here. It is a rustic place, with a restaurant and a few beds to rent.

How strange it feels. To have to change your ideas of what you are going to do. A few minutes ago, I was going to ride down a gondola to the hotel and have a nice dinner; now I am cold, with no money, in another country, and far away up a mountain. I find an interpreter, or an English speaker, and explain my situation. They're very nice, like angels, helping me. *No worry*, I think, *I will stay here, and then return to my place in the morning.* Someone thoughtfully brings, and pays for, a meal and some pivo (beer). I'm able to look at old photos of my ma on this iPad I have with me, and it's helpful in dealing with the trauma of losing her. I do not pay for anything—meal, room, or drinks.

The next morning, they feed me again, a breakfast. I thank them and start down the mountain. It's not far, only two miles. On the way down, I come across someone I know to be a mountain ranger, and he is with a Czech policeman. He points to me, and they nod. I begin to realize, *Oh my, they are looking for me.* I begin to cry (I am just a big ole baby). He checks me out to make sure I am okay. We can't communicate, so they do not know where I slept, how I slept, or what happened. Then we walk down the mountain.

The people at Bouda Máma were very alarmed because I did not return; they were required to call the police. So this set up an alert, which is why the mountain guide and policeman were looking for me. Little did I know, the policeman had already been in my apartment two hundred miles away to make sure I was not there. I later met with another policeman and he said, "Please take a phone with you next time." When I returned to Olomouc, I was told that I was on national news. "A professor from the USA was lost on top of Krkonoše mountain, but found the next day." My family in the USA did not really know, or even understand, what had happened. My Czech colleagues at the college where I work found out about it because it was on the Czech news that an American professor had gotten lost. And then I found out the guy at the Czech post office was reprimanded by the police for not taking me in.

One friend of mine wrote me this after the incident: "Hi Donny, so you had an adventure in Krkonoše, you have an adventurous mind, it's amazing how you are not lazy to go for such a walk, it's your gift, stay active and inspire others who have lost the desire for something, and remember wherever you are, there is always something that will make you happy, where you will find your desires, be happy with yourself, get rid of all fears and the universe will offer you everything you need. Misa." (I am not sure the Czech police, or the mountain ranger, or the people at Bouda Máma, would concur with Misa's nice note.)

Ugly Lessons of Travel—Victim of Crime

Spring of 2014. I had planned to drive to Bratislava to spend the weekend there. Bratislava is the capital of Slovakia, a nice historic city on the Danube. I enjoyed going there, as I had a friend working there and had visited with John and Amy before. It is not so far from Olomouc, maybe a two- to three-hour drive, with a crossing from the Czech Republic to Slovakia (half of the former Czechoslovakia). When you pass into a different country in this area, you must stop and purchase a ticket to drive on the main highway (something like our interstates). I stopped at a small place, quickly got my ticket, which cost about eight dollars, and put it on the windshield.

After about ten minutes, I began to hear something—bump, bump, bump, bump—and I thought, *What is this?* I realized my tire was flat! I had never changed a car tire in another country, but thought, *Okay, this is no big deal. I can do this.* And, having done this in the USA, it was rather easy. I took out the instruments, somewhat similar to ours, and changed the tire. Changing a tire is a concentrated matter, especially once you "jack" up the car. Once or twice I thought I had heard something, but I was focused on changing the tire because I had to get to Bratislava. I also thought I heard some loud "honk" on the highway.

It all looked okay, so I took off, and thankfully the tire was fine. About fifty minutes later, I found the hotel and I went in. I affirmed my reservation, and then returned to the car to get my money. I looked in the front seat and didn't see the pouch with my valuable things, and then I looked in the back seat and didn't even see my suitcase. I looked everywhere, but there was nothing. No passport, no money, no credit cards, no clothes, no suitcase!

I asked the lady behind the desk whether I could stay and whether they could send a bill. "No way," she said. I explained that I thought I had been robbed. Trying to calm myself down, I wondered what to do. I decided that I must get back in the car and drive back to Olomouc. But I had no money, no passport, and I needed some gas. I called a friend in Olomouc (thank you, Michal). He had a cousin there in Bratislava, and he came within twenty minutes and gave me twenty euro. I did go to the police in Slovakia and made a police report, which took longer than it should have. I left them and drove away.

It hit me when I was driving that I was singled out and robbed. Because of this crime, my plans had to be sadly altered. I began to stress, and I could feel inward strain and worry. When I passed by the area where this took place, I could see that it occurred on the Czech side, so the visit to the Slovakian police was in vain. In about two to three hours, I was back in Olomouc. I borrowed my friend's computer and was able to cancel all my credit cards. Later, I felt physically tired from all this stress, and I was sick the next day!

A few days after this, someone told me that there is a "scam or racket" on the highways, where someone will pick out a single driver and put an ice pick or knife in the tire when they leave the car for the road permit. The small puncture does not immediately make the tire flat, but once you are on the road, it will quickly go flat. When you are changing the tire, they will try to approach the car and steal what they can. They would not try to hurt you, just try to grab what they could without you knowing it. The noise I heard while changing tires was the person who punctured my tire; they had pulled up, opened my car door, and grabbed everything while I was focused on repairing the tire. I never saw them! The car horn was probably someone who saw it from the other road and was trying to alert me.

A few days later, the university received a phone call from the police in that area saying a farmer had found a suitcase belonging to a Professor Roberson located in his field. My clothes were still inside, but missing was the laptop, passport, and money. I could not believe the robbers did not want my clothes! One week later, a friend came with me and we retrieved the suitcase. Then I had to go to the embassy in Prague for a replacement passport. Lesson: when traveling alone, be careful and aware, and if you need to change a tire, call for help.

Chapter Twelve:
Bicycles, and a Dreamy Trip to Hvar

S cenario. It was 1994, and I was in Paris. I had finished a year's work and had wandered my way through Europe. From Paris, I would go by train to a ferry over the English Channel to the White Cliffs of Dover and on to London. From there, I would fly home to the USA. My focus was on leaving Paris, and I was excited to go by boat through the English Channel. I had bought the "metro" ticket to enter the subway system, and I was sort of fed up with all the little tickets and holding on to them, so once I got onto the metro, I threw my ticket away (big mistake!).

I was wandering through the labyrinth of the Paris metro system, excited to leave and move on to England. It was enough just to make it through this complicated maze and to figure out which way to go while passing thousands of people going here and there. All of a sudden, I was stopped by an official in the Paris metro asking for my ticket. I smiled and said, "Well, I bought it and entered, and I threw it away." He said, "Hand me your passport." (I was thinking what should I do because I had also been told to never, ever give up my passport . . . Should I run?) I knew I had only a few minutes to make it to the train in order to get on the boat to England for which I had reservations.

He said, "You are a problem, you have no ticket, and you must give me your passport." I could not imagine what to do. I was holding all of my luggage, and people were swarming by in large crowds, in a rush, so I got on my knees (can you believe it?) and begged him, "Sir, I am sorry. I paid for the ticket. I am not making trouble for you. I just threw it away." He was suddenly called by someone else. I could hear whistles. He looked elsewhere, and then the policeman ran in another direction. I got up, made it to the train, and then to the boat, and finally saw the White Cliffs of Dover. I learned never to throw a ticket away until you are at the absolute end of your journey.

Love of a Bicycle

When I returned to Zagreb, in 2004, one of the first things I did was purchase a bicycle. Not a fancy one, but a bike that could be ridden easily in different terrains. It served me well and greatly enhanced my life there. Zagreb is very quiet on Sunday and Saturday afternoons, and many of the crowded roads are empty. How much fun I had riding those old roads in a beautiful city. Maksimir Park is an old and historic royal forest, a little out from the city center, but a huge area of forests and trails. I loved taking my bicycle there and riding in that area. Also the river Sava is near the town of Zagreb and has a special path where you can ride a bicycle.

Eventually, I went through three bicycles—all three were stolen right from under me. One right outside my door in a dormitory setting for teachers, when I was working in Olomouc, Czech Republic. The other two were cut off the top of my car—one in Bratislava, and the other in Zagreb—and both of those were stolen while at hotels. Even in Olomouc, riding the bike was a pleasure, as there are many bicycle paths. However, for some reason, people enjoy coming up to your bicycle and seeing what they can take off. Lights, or seats, or different things attached to the bike. I was really surprised by this. People would always say, "Donald, don't leave your lights on your bike when you leave. Others will take them."

Small prayer chapel near a bike path in the Czech Republic.
Yes, that is my bicycle that eventually was stolen.

Bicycle riding is a big part of European life. Someone said to me there is a group of folks who drive through large towns at night looking for bicycles. They will cut them away from where they are, put them in a large truck, drive somewhere else, paint them, and then sell them. Not sure how true this was, but still, I am missing three bicycles.

Regardless, Europe is way beyond the USA in bicycle travel. The city of Vienna has an entire roadway just for bikes with its own lights and lanes. And, if you travel farther north, to the Netherlands and Scandinavia, the bicycle is an integral part of daily life. I saw many folks in suits riding to work as well as older women picking up groceries on the bicycle. Amsterdam is a bicycle paradise. Everyone must go to Amsterdam just to see the bicycle garages; some of them hold thousands of bikes. My last time there, I rented a bicycle every day, and easily used it to get all around the city. And there are many places in the world where the bicycle is a normal part of transport, not something relegated to children's driveways, but rather a legitimate means for how one will get to work, or school, or the store. Just recently I returned from Olomouc, and now there are rental bikes everywhere called Next Bike. They are very easy to use and free if the trip is less than thirty minutes.

Ivan and Jelena

In Zagreb, Croatia, in '93–'94, and in '96–'97, I would often eat meals in the student mensa, or cafeteria. There were several of these scattered around the city. We would buy "bonava," or meal tickets, from students who were willing to sell theirs for money. Usually, these student refugees were selling their lunch for extra money. It was very cheap, and for a great meal, we could eat for almost fifty cents. Often when I would do this, I would try to sit with someone and meet them. This is how I met Ivan and Jelena. I was intrigued by this cafeteria for students. It had two parts: one for pizza and fast food, and then one for regular meals. Thousands of students were eating here, and there were huge long lines of students everywhere. Since we were trying to meet students and begin a Christian student ministry, it was an ideal place. By the way, the food was great— real mashed potatoes, tasty meat, and other vegetables! And there was something else, special milk cartons for babies.

I met this couple this way. I asked, "May I join you? Do you speak English?" They spoke very good English and were always happy to go for a coffee. They were curious about me, and I was curious about them. They were both Croatians who were from Bosnia, and they had become refugees because of the war. He was a medical student and she was a law student. Both were very smart, had lots of energy, and were in love. We met several times, and they were always happy to meet. We all shared about our lives.

They told me the story of their experience in the war. Basically, they had three choices: (1) they could stay and perhaps be killed, (2) they could go to prison camp, or (3) they could flee. Both of their families decided to leave, and Ivan said that they could see a Serbian family moving into their home while they were driving away. I was staring at them in shock at the calm way he explained this tragic story of war. "Donald, don't worry about us," he said with a smile and a confident look. "Our people have made fortunes and lost fortunes, many times. We are not worried about this; we will be okay." I was humbled and amazed at their perspective. I am sorry I have lost touch with them.

Miloslav

Miloslav (Mila) was in the class I was teaching for PhD students. With blue eyes and bright blond hair, you could imagine him being a surfer in Southern California. Unlike many Czech people, he was smiling, happy, confident, and optimistic. He worked very hard and was one of the first people I know of to finish a PhD in three years. I went to his home in Nachod, and they even had a swimming pool! In this very cold environment, there was a pool, and it had a sliding glass top. We slept in his grandfather's former property. We played tennis, rode bikes in the area, and took a tour of old rock formations. We even joined his father and their friends for a sauna. Mila's story encompasses some of the interesting history of this era. During the great days of Czechoslovakia, Mila's family did well, due to his grandfather who had two grocery stores. His grandfather worked hard and made some money. However, after the Nazis came, and then the communists, Mr. Klugar's store was taken from him, and he was forced to work for someone else in his own grocery store! After the fall of communism, Mila's father was quick to go to the authorities and to purchase or reinstate all the property that had been taken by the state. And now the Klugar grocery stores are back in effect. Mila married another PhD student, Jitka; they continue to be involved in medical research in the Czech Republic. (Even more interesting is that the family has recently sold the grocery stores to immigrants from China!)

A Dreamy, but Real, Trip

A new sleek train had arrived in Zagreb. Something new and fresh, not with the lingering smells and looks of World War II, or the communist era. This specially built train from Italy was fast and modern, and it was the newest thing in Croatia. I happily boarded the train with my packed lunch, grabbed from leftovers in the kitchen, and my suitcase. The elegantly carved rivers of green, brown, and blue of the water rushing around the limestone in the mountains created a beautiful background for the ride. Passing countless honey and cheese vendors, soon one could see the majestic Plitvička Jezera. Steady streams of water cutting and carving through the limestone, creating fiction-like pools of turquoise. Soon we were gaining in elevation and passing through the dense and lush forests of the Lika region, and eventually, we ascended over the mountains of the Velebit. The appearance of the Adriatic always takes one's breath away, the endless dynamic of a sea or ocean somehow touches the soul deep inside, sort of reminding us there is an eternity somewhere.

As the train landed in Split, we were surrounded by a bunch of older women, most of them had aprons on or something on their head, the elderly and responsible matrons of homes all around the area holding up signs in English. "Come home with me" for twenty dollars, or "room for rent" for thirty-five dollars including dinner, on and on and on. I looked at one nice lady, and I knew how to say, "Gdje?" (Where?), and she showed me on the map. It wasn't far, just outside the walls of the ancient city of Split. Next day, I would catch the ferry to the island of Hvar.

Like a lamb led to slaughter, I simply followed this stalwart woman as she took us through the small paths within the leftovers of Diocletian's

Palace. Instead of Roman soldiers guarding the delusional Diocletian, I was going to take a room with a capitalistic Yugoslav woman. The room was comfortable, simply a bed, and a bathroom down the hall (the only bathroom in the home). I left for a walk about the former palace of the Roman emperor, now restored into the remains of Split, Croatia. I was shocked by the sidewalks and pathways made of marble that are left from the work of the emperor's slaves. Today this recreated urban area is lined with small shops and restaurants. Some parts of the palace were divided into museums and churches; cars are parked outside of the old town area.

After a breakfast of scrambled eggs, bread, butter, and a coffee made by my host, I thanked her ("Hvala") and went in search of my boat. Outside the palace is the old port of Split, still active with large ships, mainly from the national ship ferry line—Jadrolinija. They take folks to all of the islands in various directions. My ship left at twelve and arrived in Staro Mesto in one to two hours on the island of Hvar.

Hvar town center is a lovely place to spend the evening after the sun sets.
It is so interesting to watch folks crisscross in the center,
hurrying to their various activities.

I felt as if I had been on a voyage of the Odyssey with Homer himself—walking off the ship with turquoise glimmering water all around. I waited a few minutes for a bus to take us to the other side of the island, and the town of Hvar, on the island Hvar (Hvar, Hvar, Croatia). The newly built tunnel got us there quickly, and I was thankful for this progress. The older road was a curvy, long, slow approach over the top of the mountain to the other side of the island.

I walked on the ancient walkways of limestone to the Tourist Information office and asked if they could help me find a room. The woman there called several people (all of whom she knew), and eventually another older woman showed up and took me home. For twenty-five dollars a night, I had a small singe room in their home, a former attic converted into money-making tourist lofts. It was enough for me. I was again in Hvar and willing to put up with the noise of folks nearby. After organizing my room, I put on my walking shoes and bathing suit and threw a book or two in my backpack and some money.

I meandered around the sea town, walking in the same places that the ancient mariners trod. In the shadow it was cool, but in the sun, it was intensely hot. The small walking paths through the town were like a maze in a game. Each corner brought me face-to-face with blooming bright-colored flowers and plants, and off in the distance, I could always see the sharp blue of the Adriatic. Wet clothes were strung out from window to opposite building, creating a colorful pathway along the top of the buildings, and a natural drying. Near the center of Hvar was a harbor with various coves inside, and a lot of boats. The center of the town was full of activity, people watching, and folks going through the town, looking for food or drink, or meeting someone. The place was a cornucopia of color, lavender, boats, and water. I had never seen anything like it, and I was trance-like walking around the area, absorbing it all, totally entertained. Children selling small shells they had collected, or boys playing fudbal on the sidewalks, or people playing water polo in the harbor—everywhere you turned there was expression of life.

This local is selling various forms of lavender from their family farm. The hills of Hvar and its coastal location make it an ideal place for growing lavender. In the right location, you can find endless hills of fragrant purple lavender stretching to the Adriatic.

There are hardly any sandy beaches, so someone told me to take a boat from the center of town to one of the islands. He pointed to a nearby small island. The next morning, I stopped by a grocery and market and bought some food and drink for the day, and I paid a man the equivalent of four dollars to take me in his small boat over to the island. We waited until enough people were in the boat to satisfy the owner. Eventually, I was on a fifteen-minute excursion on the beautiful Adriatic. I found out there is a string of islands where you can take these boats for a quieter and more natural experience. I walked around the island, jumped into the water to cool off, and later in the day, I caught the boat back to Hvar (once an hour). The pine trees hugging the coast create a wonderful clash of green and blue color with the water. In this area, water shoes are a must, beaches are rare, and you often have to walk and swim near sharp rocks.

INTERPOL

Chapter Thirteen:
International Police

Branimir

I met Branimir at the University of Zagreb while he was a student. He invited me to come home with him one weekend, and I wanted to see the real life of the people I had met, so I went. This was in 1994, toward the end of the Yugoslav Wars. Normally, it is a two- to three-hour train ride to Slavonski Brod; however, the Serbian forces had destroyed/cut the train line. So this meant the train had to make a slow detour to get there, and it ended up taking five to six hours.

The train station looked like it was being held together by large pieces of tape. There were cracks in the floors and walkways of the station area, and on the large windows on the front, there was tape on the damaged windows, caused by shelling. Everywhere were those sandbags that are used in dangerous situations. I thought that this place must be in some type of danger. I arrived at their home and met his parents. They were so kind and helpful. We got in a car and went to an area near a hill where there was a small house, which they called a "weekend house." This is very common in Croatia and the Czech Republic, where you have a simple one-room house just to get away from the town and your normal living situation. It is almost like camping out, but you are in a rustic shelter. Surrounded by a garden, vegetable and flower, it can be a very restful oasis.

I met his sister, her husband, and their children. And we walked around the town, which is also on the border of a Serbian area of Bosnia. The next day we were walking on the dike area near the river, a high ridge to keep the Sava River in its banks in case of flooding, when Branimir said, "Donald, let's get down from this ledge. You have on a red sweater, and snipers have been known to keep picking off people." I calmly walked down the incline from the bank of the river, thinking, *Wow.* At the back of their house was a small garden with a place for sitting, like a picnic table, that was covered with some vine. They were offering homemade wine and homemade "slivovica," a type of brandy made from their own fruit.

When we retired for the day, in my room, I saw a small hole in the wall near my pillow. I pointed this out to Branimir. He said, "During the shelling of Slavonski Brod, a piece of shrapnel flew through this. It could have killed me." (Imagine my thoughts as I tried to sleep.) At this time, the Serbian troops were only a few miles away, but he assured me there was some sort of ceasefire in the fighting. I returned several times over the years that I was living in Croatia. His parents were always so kind, and his mother was always in the kitchen cooking up some tasty food, especially Bosnian. She was from Bosnia and had married a Croat, Branimir's father, and they made their home in Slavonski Brod. Branimir said that during the war, there were at one time twenty folks living in their home since they had to flee the war within Bosnia. I was amazed at their kindness to me, their happiness despite a war, and the food that came out of that kitchen. And his dad was such a fun guy, who could drink a lot of the slivovica and would spend all day working in his garden. Most people would never go to visit Slavonski Brod, but it's a lovely town, situated on the Sava River, next to Bosnia and Herzegovina, and there is an old Austro-Hungarian fort left from the previous regime.

International Police

Fall of 2007. If you have traveled internationally, you will notice that when you check into the place where you are staying, you usually present a passport or identification. All of this is to register you with the police department so they can keep up with you while you are there. This is so that before you leave the country, if there are any remaining charges to your name, they will stop you at the border and you will pay them. Sometimes all of this is mistaken for high-level espionage, or spying, something like in the Cold War, but mainly it's about money. However, if you have broken their laws, and they are looking for you, they may be able to find you this way.

Most tourists have one to three months' permission to stay within the country. However, if you are going to stay longer, then you need a more permanent visa, which is permission by the government to stay. This enables them to track you if necessary but also to obtain some payment for the use of the public facilities and services of that country. For example, you must help to pay for sidewalks, or roads, or lighting at night, or a police force if you will be staying for so long. Now there are other situations, where politically, or religiously, they may not want you to remain in their country. Always check with the US Department of State if you are in question about any country.

In my situation when I was living there, it was for an indefinite period of time. This became complicated. There is a special international police set up to check on foreigners in the country. I had to show them a contract from the university for my employment and for my housing. Then I would have some sort of interview or discussion, and all of the material would go though some reviewers. For sure, they checked my name for any possible crime, or danger, or potential problems. When I returned in one month, I had to go to a post office and purchase some sort of "stamp," that was worth $200 and place it on the form. (I could never understand why they didn't have these stamps at the police station.)

Every time my contract renewed, I had to repeat this process. Later, the last six years I was there, the office shifted to another town, in a bright shiny new building, with all new people. Sometimes an officer working there would look at me and say, "Please speak Czech. You are in Czech." Yet, I was treated very well there, and it looked as if all the other people wanting permission to live there were treated fairly. The hallway outside the office looked like an international ensemble—lots of people from around the world wanting to live in the Czech Republic. The permission of the government also meant I could use their medical card, which paid for all medical issues.

EUROPE

Chapter Fourteen:

First Trip through Europe

Scenario. Winter of 1994. There is a great amount of freedom and fun to train travel. It is so nice to leave the driving to someone else, to be able to relax, sit, read, or eat while riding through the countryside. The train station is its own community with a variety of stores and everyone in anticipation of a trip. Some countries "do" trains better than others—Switzerland and Germany, for sure. One interesting experience was riding the beautiful, compact, "toy-like" Swiss train at the Bernese Oberland. I felt like Heidi would be waiting for me at the end. Every small town in this region of Switzerland had these special trains going back and forth. In order to use the trains, you must know where you are going, write it down, give it to the person selling tickets, and get the time and location of the train. But overall, it's out of your control. Someone else is driving, others are being assigned to sit next to you, and people you don't know are also on the train.

The School of Travel offers a class in European history, travel, geography, and weather. It's a short course of ten days, and you will learn details about Spain, Switzerland, France, Belgium, Germany, and the Netherlands.

Although I thoroughly enjoyed this trip, I would never repeat it. It was too quick and straining, and it involved sleeping for two nights on a train seat. For an introduction to Europe, this trip was okay for a young person with lots of energy and patience. I took one small bag that I could carry over my shoulder and a small backpack. For souvenirs, I only bought postcards (one from each place). I bought the expensive Eurail Pass in the USA, which puts you in first class. (This is really not necessary, as second-class train travel in Europe is fine.) First class separates you from most of the people, and the others riding there are usually other Americans who have done the same. This was some sort of a tourist promotion that a lot of Americans bought. All in all, it was a great introduction to Europe. I had to learn how to survive on the road, that you can find good food in a grocery store (yogurt and fruit are the easiest), how to follow directions and ask questions politely, how to keep track of my passport, money, and tickets, and how to be adaptable. It was also a trip of great freedom. I found friendly people everywhere who also spoke English. No worries, I could go where I wanted. It was emotional for me to leave the USA and my mom, as I really felt I was cutting ties with a previous way of life. This trip helped me to relax, enjoy the moment, and process all that was going on in my mind. I would never be the same again.

A Whirlwind Trip (Don't Do This Again)

September of 1993. I had decided I would go on a trip through some of the popular places in Europe before I began the year in Zagreb, Croatia.

So I planned in my schedule to leave two weeks earlier than the date that I was to arrive for training program in Budapest, Hungary. I had a lot to prepare for, not only for the year in Croatia but also for an extra two-week travel trip beforehand. Where should I go and what should I do? Mother suggested I talk to her friend Nell. Nell and her husband, Bill, had traveled extensively in Europe. She had set up all their trips and knew where to go and what to do. The only difference was they were first-class travelers, and I had a very low budget.

We met and talked and she gave me a small brochure about travel in Europe. Mainly she encouraged me to go and see this beautiful part of the world. She helped to give me the confidence that I could do this, and that it was worth doing. I bought a train pass called the Eurail Pass for two weeks, and I made a tentative plan of what places I would go to. I had no hotel reservations. With help from Nell, we planned what cities to go to, but I decided I would get the hotels and places to stay once I arrived. I rationalized that I was going to a large city, and I would just walk up to some hotel and see whether they had a room, and if not, I would try the next one. (Basically, I was too focused on spending fourteen months in Croatia, and I did not have the time or patience to line up and get in touch with hotels all over Europe.) I was both excited and scared, especially doing this adventure on my own.

Frankfurt. The plane landed in Frankfurt, and I had two very large suitcases, weighing sixty or so pounds each, and within one of them was hidden $4,000. These two large suitcases I left at a luggage checking station. Most all train stations have something like this, a "left luggage" area—some place to leave suitcases, where you can pick them up in one hour, or more. I left my suitcases for ten days. (Some of this has changed since 9/11.) And I took one small bag already prepared for this two-week trip, which contained only the bare minimum of clothes. Two pairs of shoes (one of these was on my feet), four shirts, four pairs of underwear, four pairs of socks, four T-shirts, two pairs of pants, a journal, and a small Bible.

I would make a circle of western Europe, return here, gather these two large suitcases, and get on the train east to Budapest. I had written down a plan or itinerary—land in Frankfurt, go to Amsterdam, Brussels, Paris, Barcelona, Swiss Alps, then back to Frankfurt. It was an ambitious plan to try on one's own in ten days. I knew I did not have the space, or the money, for souvenirs, so the only souvenir I would get from each place would be one postcard. I would eat as cheaply as possible, avoiding restaurants.

Amsterdam. After flying on the plane, checking the bags, getting on the train, and activating the Eurail Pass (put me in first class), I could relax and watch the scenery. I somewhat dozed after the overnight flight and emotional departure from family, and then the quick transition that needed to take place in Frankfurt airport. I just sat and stared out the window of the train going to Amsterdam. There were many bicycle paths, and I saw someone in a suit riding a bicycle to work. I was literally a neophyte traveler, having no idea of where I was going or what I would do except get off the train in Amsterdam and find a hotel. After stopping in Amsterdam, I just walked outside the train station, and there was some friendly guy handing out fliers to a hotel. Outside the train station, I could tell I was on a different planet, or world, or continent— not only was the train station shockingly beautiful, but the smells, the wind, the city all were flooding my mind with new sensations. I followed the directions to the hotel. His brother was the manager and had rooms above the restaurant area. I simply trusted them. Like many buildings in Amsterdam, it was very small and very old. When I got to my room, I took everything out of my little bag and just stared at it. I thought how amazing it was that my life had been reduced to these twenty or so items. Most important was to keep track of significant documents, mainly passport and money. I just walked around the old part of the town. The next morning, the manager suggested I take a boat ride in the canals of Amsterdam. I did this and was amazed by all the water and the old homes built around the canals. And then I left for the next destination. With the Eurail Pass, you could leave when you wanted; it was an open ticket.

Brussels. For some reason, I had heard about Brussels all of my life and went there next. (Riding a train from city to city, I spoke to an older woman who was sitting in my cabin. She was friendly and we exchanged addresses, and we corresponded during this year in Croatia. Eventually, I met her and her family in Bordeaux, France.) I walked around the old town and found a hotel just by walking up to one and getting a room. Here is a beautiful ornate old town square, and the famous statue of the little boy who happens to be urinating. It is called "Manneken Pis." Later I would see other versions of this small boy urinating with glee in many public gardens. As I left the next morning for Paris, I was surprised that outside of the tourist area, I saw a lot of graffiti and dirty streets—the typical urban dilemma.

Paris. The place I thought I was going to stay in Paris did not work out, and I was sent to another hotel for tourists. I stayed there two nights and enjoyed it so much. It was an inexpensive hotel designed for low-budget travelers. A very small room, with a bathroom, so small that the shower was just part of the bathroom; the nozzle was above the top of the sink and the entire bathroom was in the shower.

I walked around Paris learning how to manage the subway, which could be very complicated for someone like me who was not used to such. With eagerness, I went to the center and found Notre-Dame; it was amazing to see it for the first time. Coming face-to-face with something you have heard about all of your life—well, it's somewhat inspiring to see it in person. How often had I seen a picture of Notre-Dame, or the Eiffel Tower, or the *Mona Lisa*—in countless stories, documentaries, or books? Seeing them in real life, the authenticity of a moment, it's hard to explain. This confirmation of the past affirms previous stories and sort of welcomes the traveler into the real world. The next day, I toured the Louvre Art Museum and saw the famous *Mona Lisa*. Like other travelers, one must go there and pay her homage. I was surprised by the number of people who asked me whether I had seen it, or even assumed that I had seen it. It was sort of like a game. When you enter the Louvre, you see signs saying, "*Mona Lisa* this way." Regardless, I also followed the others like mice chasing some bit of cheese, through the mazes of the museum, and eventually there she was and with everyone else! After walking up and looking at this familiar painting, I turned to the others who were also looking. This became even more interesting, and it was the inspiration for later research on the impact of a museum. Other museums were equally tantalizing, especially the Musée d'Orsay. I loved Paris, its history, shops, delicatessens and bakeries, and coffee from the sidewalk cafés. Keep in mind, I refused to buy anything because of my budget, ate at McDonald's or grocery stores, and only bought one post-card from each town. But I was loving this adventure. It was so much fun. Each day I felt more confident, more relaxed, and I was learning how to travel in this particular way. To be away from home, like a bird leaving a nest, can be an unsettling situation. But I had changed; now I felt completely confident in the unknown, with strange faces all around me, unknown languages in my ear, and without a clue of how to get around, or how to count the money in my pocket. This confidence was a sense of deep, even spiritual, inward peace, that all was right, all was okay. I was growing in confidence in another country and for the purpose for which I was intended.

Barcelona. I left Paris and realized the only way I could make it to Barcelona was to take an overnight train. I had a layover in Lyon, France, and walked around the town for a few hours. Then I got on a train through the night to Barcelona. It was not a sleeper car, just an overnight train, but your seat did recline some. Barcelona was huge and different. I walked around some of the town and wanted to get to the Mediterranean

Sea. I found a way to take a subway near the beach and jumped into the Mediterranean for the first time. Barcelona also had unique architecture, mainly the influence of the architect Gaudí. Later in the day, I had to get back on the train overnight to get to Switzerland.

Switzerland. I got off the train in Geneva, Switzerland, and needed to wash clothes. I got out of the station and found some "wash place," and washed all the clothes I could. Then I took the train to the area of Interlaken where there are two famous lakes and the impressive Swiss mountains. But it was not the Switzerland I wanted to see, so I referred to the book Nell had given me, and it said to go to Grindelwald. So, I headed there and found my place. I stayed in a youth hostel for two nights, loving every moment of this alpine heaven. I was hiking, walking in the high Alps—the Bernese Oberland, such amazing beauty. High mountains, glaciers, valleys, waterfalls, hiking paths, classic mountain trains taking you from place to place—overall jaw-dropping, finger-pointing, alluring creation. One brochure Nell had given me explained about youth hostels, I found a youth hostel in Grindelwald. For young travelers (I think I was thirty-nine), this was budget travel, in a dormitory setting, with rooms for eight to twenty people, and the price was about eighteen dollars per night and included a breakfast. A place that encouraged interaction and meeting new people. It was everything I could imagine, and perhaps at this time, the only way I could afford to travel in Europe.

I began to see that I could get around Europe in an easy and affordable way. I learned I could trust people. It was like gaining a new hobby, the future possibility of travel. The world seemed to be a smaller and friendlier place. And I saw I could survive okay on my own without anyone for a while.

Frankfurt. I arrived in Frankfurt, got my two large bags (they were okay and the $4,000 was safe), and took another all-night train to Budapest. My two-week journey of personal indulgence had ended. Now I was going to work and to meet the "powers that be" with the Campus Crusade program in Hungary. This seminar was so we could learn what we needed for this one-and-half-year program in Croatia. It was also a transition to leave the independence of traveling alone, to be with other Americans. Ah, life is daily full of transitions and adaptations.

Budapest. We were in Budapest for about five days preparing for our upcoming year in Croatia. The Danube River goes through the middle of Budapest; one side is Buda, and the other, Pest. There were many beautiful buildings rebuilt after World War II, and some amazing museums, including the Hungarian National Gallery, Museum of Fine Arts, Jewish Synagogue (called The Great Synogogue of Budapest), the Hungarian State Opera house, and a historic tram line going to a beautiful park. Budapest is also famous for many hot springs that are fun to go to. The language of Hungary is so different from anything I had ever heard or seen, and Budapest was uniquely different from western Europe.

Distracted Travel

Traveling to new places takes one to the unfamiliar. This allows for all types of new information to hit the traveler on all sides. New faces, food, smells, geography and botany, language, maps, and transit. All of this can lead to a sort of sensory overload. Now, if one is traveling with a group, and there is a travel guide, this usually does not happen. However, with independent travel where the traveler is always in charge then everything is in the hands of the traveler.

I have had pockets full of different coins, paper money, and transport tickets. These must be continuously dealt with, or you will quickly get discombobulated! Also, if you are using public transport, you have to have the travel ticket ready to show the driver or police control. Losing things, leaving things! I have left scarves and hats all over the world, as well as many other objects, simply because for some reason, I was distracted during the travel. The point being, the world uses tickets, coins, and schedules that we are not used to; this can be very distracting, resulting in a loss of focus.

How to Engage with Strangers

1. Do not be overly friendly.
2. With a relaxed, calm face, ask politely and quietly, "Do you speak English?"
3. Ask them, "May I join you?" (If they say no, or move away; it's okay, let them go.)
4. Start off with something like: "My name is _____. I am traveling in your country, and I wanted to meet some local people or other travelers. Do you have a few minutes to tell me about your country?"
5. And listen to them; do not correct, or laugh at them, or interject words into their broken English. Just nod and take in this miniature United Nations.
6. Be comfortable with silence, and do not feel you have to be speaking all of the time.
7. They will be curious about you, but let them ask you questions. (Don't say too much. Americans have a tendency to tell strangers everything about themselves.)
8. If all goes well, then you can suggest exchanging email addresses. I think that is the easiest and least threatening way.
9. Later, if you want to continue this relationship, email them and suggest meeting again, and then see where it goes from there. I am in contact with many folks, ones that I met in these ways.

Chapter Fifteen:

Zagreb and Croatia

S cenario. We met a lot of refugees from Yugoslavia while in Zagreb. The country had been invaded by Serbia; many people came to Zagreb for safety. One student, Marko, was very friendly, and he wanted to meet Americans and speak English. We had a small "party" or gathering and invited students, and while we were talking and eating, most of the Yugoslavs were smoking and drinking (well, they were college students). Marko had two cigarettes in his mouth. I had never seen this before. He said to me, "Donald, you must understand. We are very nervous. There is a war here."

Everyday Experiences in Zagreb and Croatia

The School of Travel offers a special class on the former Yugoslavia. This class will take you from Serbia to another country, Croatia. And like before, you will learn the unique history, geography, way of living, and culture of this area, and specifically the capital city of Zagreb. I will share with you some of the main aspects of living in Zagreb, Croatia.

Zagreb. For some reason, based in Middle Ages history, there is a military cannon that goes off every day in the middle of the city of Zagreb. This loud cannon is a reminder to the folks of Zagreb of how they beat someone in some ancient battle (relating to defending themselves from the Ottomans). Remembering the recent war, the first time I heard it, I yelled and jumped in the air. So you can imagine the fun we had with visitors, or friends that came. We would bring up the recent war, and make sure they were very close to this cannon during that time at noon. Zagreb is a fascinating city, with three distinct parts—the old medieval part, the part with Austro-Hungarian influence, and the new Zagreb with its modern communist design. This capital city is often overlooked by folks eager to get to the coast, but for us it was like a giant playground just waiting to be enjoyed and discovered.

In Zagreb, there is a well-known open market called Dolac. Everything you need for food can be bought in this amazing market. All products are fresh and often brought by nearby older women with dirt still on the carrots. The seafood market is also full of fresh fish directly from the sea.

Language and numbers. "Ah Donald, I really like to see the ring on your toe. It's really beautiful. Is it something special?" (In the world of languages, often the words for toes and fingers are used interchangeably.) The fascination of language resulted in a continuous laugh, and it helped to make every day more fun. They loved to hear a clear American accent, and even more so if you had something unique, such as a Southern accent, and they would enjoy talking with you. I never knew that you could be so creative with letters of the alphabet! Or maybe I just thought every alphabet was just like ours. And the numbers 0–9, they wrote out the 1, 2, 4, 7 in a different way than what I was used to. Time is often military time—14:22 instead of 2:22 p.m.; and when you write the date, they always put the month second, and the day first—10. 9. 20 is September 10, 2020. All of this added to the fun and enjoyment and sometimes the confusion.

Keys, locks, and doors. Around the world, there are different keys, doors, and locks, and I had to learn this quickly. In Croatia and in the Czech Republic, the homes have doors with many locks. I have never figured out why because crime is very low. But I was used to the American doors, which do not automatically lock. However most doors in Europe will lock if you close them, so you better have your key with you. The solution is to

Some folks in the nicer older homes have beautifully carved and crafted doors.

keep the key in the keyhole from the inside, so you will remember to take it with you. However, you should never push it all the way in because one time, even though the key was in the door, I did not remove it to take it with me, and I had pushed it all the way in. The owner's key could not come through the door because my key was on the other side; thus, we had to call the expensive key guy to come and solve the problem. So the solution is, when you come in, you immediately put your key partially in the lock, and close the door. Many of the flats that I visited had a very thick door, maybe for the weather? And on the side of the door, there were not just two locks, but many times there would be three or four!

Police presence. There was often a police or military presence at most public events, and especially at soccer or fudbal games, there could be hundreds of police officers. Knowing that Croatia was currently at war with Serbia, we were careful while around these police officers. One rumor I heard was that the Yugoslav Wars actually started at a "fudbal" match! There would also be a lot of guns, and machine guns, on the police in large airports in Europe. I thought about what a funny contrast it was, that in the USA with all of its guns, there are no police walking with guns in US airports, whereas in some parts of Europe, you see police officers with large guns everywhere. There seemed to be a larger presence of police. Police for the road, police for local affairs, and then other police for international issues. In huge contrast to our state patrol, the police on the streets would stand next to the road and hold up a small sign with "stop" on it. That was their version of the state patrol officer chasing you down in a fast car!

Smile. No one is smiling in central Europe. Even when you say "Smile" or "Cheese" when you are taking a picture, no one smiles. While in our country we are taught to smile at strangers, over there, they think it is strange to try to engage with strangers. One of my co-professors one day said to me, "Donald, quit smiling. I am so tired of these Americans everywhere smiling at everyone." I know this also may be because I was raised in a friendly small town in the South.

Public toilets. When you use the public toilets, you have to pay something. This took me a long time to learn, and many times I would be chased by a lady in charge for not paying something. And by the way, toilet paper is usually extra. So if you don't get your toilet paper at the beginning, then . . . ! (On a more recent trip, I noticed in many bathrooms that there is not an attendant.) We saw a variety of commodes, ones with strings that allowed water to rush down a pipe, some toilets with no place to sit, and others with only a platform to squat down.

Dark rooms and hallways. Electricity is expensive in this part of the world. So, there are not as many streetlights at night or lighting in public places. Usually, when you enter a building where someone lives, it is completely dark, and you may see a little button with a small red light in it. Once you press it, you have lights for about eight minutes. Many homes only have lights on within the room they are using.

Not having a car. I was with a group of eight, and of course, in the USA we all had cars. So, we learned to use public transportation, to wait, and to sit with others we didn't know. At first, it was like playing, riding these cute electric trams. It was like we were stepping inside some childhood toys. And often, we were sort of playing, laughing, hanging on to various bars. One day, I rested my feet up on the seat in front of me (a very bad American habit), and this cute child ran over to me and shook her finger in my face. Adding to this was the public train system, which is very extensive. We learned to enjoy it, and it was great to go on some trip and be able to take a picnic, or books to read. I began to realize how a car separates you from others. A car is really so convenient, possibly even to the point of indulgence. You can drive yourself, go as fast or slow as you want, insulate yourself with a level of temperature, as well as enjoy your own choice of music. When you catch the tram, or bus, you are joining together with other people. You are making an instant community. Also you are waiting on someone else to drive. You may be cold or hot depending on the weather.

Being far from home and friends. Although we did miss everyone at home, we knew that we were only there for about fourteen months. That is not so long when you are with eight other wonderful and fun folks. In fact, most of us were never homesick, and we started to love being there. We created a small community where the eight of us came together to encourage and help each other. We would get letters from family and friends saying how much they knew we were suffering and having a hard time and how they were concerned and praying for us. We couldn't help but laugh at this misunderstanding. Perhaps this was their hope that we were not okay away from home and wanted to return quickly. Instead, although we were in a far away place, which also was having war in various parts of the country, we were adjusting and learning how to have a great time. Some of this misunderstanding was possibly due to the overreporting of news about the breakup of Yugoslavia and the subsequent war, which was taking place while we were there. Showing how misunderstood many of these issues are, at the same time, the worst genocide in African history was taking place in Rwanda, and there was a lack of attention on this in international news.

The drive from Zagreb to the coast of Croatia is full of adventure and wonder. One example is this hobbit-like town—Slunj, Croatia—where pools of water cascade through the limestone. It is certainly worth a stop, and of course, a coffee.

Issues of language. At this time, the world wanted to learn to speak English. Is there some explanation for this? Somehow, the English language had become the internationally accepted speech, especially in sports, business, medicine, technical books, politics, and academics. So it was easy for us to meet folks and to speak English, but only with those who had a need to learn English. Although we were trying to learn some Croatian language, most of them would rather practice their English with us. The only way for us to get a visa to remain there for a year was to pretend to be Croatian language students. The entire study of language is a lot of fun. And this made it even easier for us to meet people, as everyone wanted to come to our "get-togethers" to practice English. For example, how did "Bok," a derivative of Bog, meaning God, become the informal greeting for hello in Croatia? Consonants are preferred over vowels, and every letter is pronounced. We all learned the importance of really listening and speaking clearly. And, if you wanted to communicate clearly, you needed to drop idioms, such as "Something is fishy here" or "Well, I am just fit to be tied," as well as your accent. This was very easy to do—simply drop the accent, speak like a news reporter, speak slowly, and do not use any of your own local expressions, like "Honeychild," "Isn't that wicked," "That is as loud as a drum," "Alligator tears," etc.

The influence of American culture. I thought going to Europe that I would see some avant-garde European movies, but every time we went to a movie, it was always an American film. There is a huge influence of American culture, especially music, MTV, television, and movies. I heard more music from Michal Jackson, REM, and Prince than I had ever heard in my life there. This also was a great advantage for us. I always wanted to hear local, traditional music; and some of the Croatian students who were into music knew more about American music than I did.

The coastline of Croatia. The first time I saw the coast, I could not believe the contrast between the mountains on the coast and the Adriatic Sea. The color of the water is turquoise, and there are around 1,100 islands from one end to the other. It was like there were two countries: interior Croatia, which is very central European, then the coast on the Adriatic Sea, which is very Mediterranean. Also, there are many very old towns on these islands, with beautiful intact architecture and well-preserved buildings. Some of these towns have become their own travel destination—Korčula, Hvar, or Mali Lošinj. The locals are very friendly to nice tourists. They want your money, so they will welcome you and give you some amazing fresh food from the Adriatic. Travel and tourism is a large industry in Croatia. This country has emerged from the socialist perspective of Yugoslavia, but it depends on financial gain from tourism. You can understand why Serbia did not want this country to leave the former Yugoslavia with its beautiful and enticing coastline. Interestingly, there are not so many sandy beaches, as we are used to in the USA, rather they are rockier, requiring shoes, and you must take care around the rocks. Each part of Croatia is so fun to explore—Istria, Slavonia, Zagreb, the interior area around Gospić, and the coastline from Dubrovnik to Pula. Plitvička Jezera National Park is one of the greatest wonders I have ever seen.

I have visited many national parks, and Plitvička Jezera is one of the most beautiful. Mountains and water combine to create a unique place of wonder.

Chapter Sixteen:

Life in the Czech Republic and Olomouc

I want to introduce you to two folks I met in the Czech Republic.

Jana

Fall of 2007. I met Jana at the university. She was also a teacher and a researcher. I knew that she was serious about her work, so I asked her if we could work on a research project together. It was a combination of quantitative and qualitative research on seniors. This work brought us closer together and we became friends. She invited me to visit her family at their home: her three children and her husband, Marek. They were both athletes, teachers, and parents. And also like me, they both take faith seriously and were active in church with their children and with the fellowship of other younger parents. Jana's family, like many in this area of central Europe, was a collection of people from all over, including her grandmother who was Jewish Russian. I also became friends with Jana's father, Ivan, and visited him and his wife in their town of Třebíč. He is close to my age and very active, a great example of positive aging. He took me to their garden, and then their weekend house. He also was very interesting to talk with, and we could discuss several topics. This to me was so interesting! Although an atheist, he and I also discussed faith and what it means to be a believer. He showed me the town of Třebíč and its well-known historical area. He is an avid gardener. They have the weekend house outside of town as well as a garden in a garden colony with others.

Marek's family (Jana's husband) also has a garden/weekend house in the hills near Olomouc. Marek would often ride his bicycle to his school where he taught physical education. Often on Easter, I would go to their home and eat the carefully prepared food for Easter with their family. Like most folks in the Czech Republic, they bought an older place and repaired it themselves for their home. In the kitchen area, there is a ceramic wood stove that you could lie on. It was like part of the furniture and traditional in this part of central Europe. It is like a woodburning stove inserted into a ceramic counter, and on top of the counter, you can sit or lie down. I look forward to seeing them soon.

Michal

Fall of 2007. I met Michal at the mensa (cafeteria at the college) in Olomouc. We were just saying hello as we were in the line, and I thought, *This young man knows English very well.* I asked him whether I could join him. I found out he had spent time at Valdosta State University, which was only twenty-five miles from my home in the USA. We had a lot in common, and he wanted to speak English with a native speaker.

I taught him how to play backgammon, and we had many fun evenings drinking pivo and playing a competition of backgammon, as well as listening to some music and solving all the problems of the world. Michal and I became comfortable around each other and trusted each other. So we spent a lot of time together. I would often let him use my car when I was in the USA. We made several trips together, and he invited me to do many things with his family. I saw how the people in this area were willing to become very close to you if they trusted you. His father had taught physical education, and his mother had worked in a business. They raised three children who became a successful part of this new Czech Republic world. Interestingly, his sister had a tennis scholarship at Kansas State! I also became close with his brother Vlastic and his family. And I would spend time with them on their property, which was near Litovel, about ten miles from Olomouc. I loved to see their garden and how his father-in-law, Jiri, would work wonders with the soil. Gardening is a large part of the lives of many folks who live outside of the larger towns. Family is a significant aspect of the fabric of this culture—keeping close to each other, helping parents and grandparents. Many times, several generations live together in one home. When I first met Vlastic, he and his wife and children were living in the same house as her parents. A few years later, they built a home together, but at that time, there were two separate houses, yet they were joined, and they shared the same garden, barn, and yard. They seemed very happy together. I thought, *What a great way to live one's life.*

Daily Life in the Czech Republic

Scenario. Fall of 2007. A colleague at the university in the Czech Republic had told me he had to go home to play in a basketball game. I invited myself to come and see how sport works in this area of the world. He explained to me the roads to take (before GPS) and where to go. It took about an hour and a lot of curvy driving on small unfamiliar roads. I arrived at a gymnasium/sports hall and went inside. It was Sunday morning at 10 a.m. For me, what a surprising time for a community basketball game. There were two teams from different towns playing in this organized basketball competition, which is all over the Czech Republic (which some are now calling Czechia). I was among four fans in the stands, and I was the only person who had driven from out of town to see this basketball match! I was prepared to drive back after the game, but Michal invited me to join his family for lunch. I met his parents and ate a typical Czech lunch—soup, meat and vegetables with potatoes. I could not speak with his parents, so he translated everything, and it was so interesting to be inside a "typical" Czech family home. It was in a large building with other families; six stories with three flats on each floor. Each flat had one bathroom for everyone, a small working patio (for mops and clothes, etc.), a small kitchen, one sitting room, and one or two bedrooms. Also, every room in that building was the same. I felt a lot of love and ate such great food.

The school of travel offered for me an advanced class lasting twenty years. During this time, I learned the details of working and living in the Czech Republic as well as Croatia; this included culinary specialties, language, history (with special emphasis on Nazis and Communists), and interaction with locals. Although there are a lot of similarities, there are also some interesting differences.

Clothes washers. September of 2007. The first few years I lived in the Czech Republic, I lived in an international facility for students and teachers. My first-time washing clothes, the busy staff did not have time to explain how to use the machine. Finally, I just asked someone to come and show me. The normal amount of time to wash a load of clothes is 2.5 hours, a very slow, hot water process where the clothes become very clean. The clothes slowly go round and round and round, yet changing directions. How can it be so different in the USA? Our normal wash cycle is 25–30 minutes, and our clothes are clean because of an "agitator" that moves around and up and down with the clothes, agitating the dirt away. What does this say about us all? Is it possible that our inventions also reflect something about our culture? From my perspective, the European washers are smaller, use less water than we do, and take longer time. Americans (USA) don't mind agitation, aggressiveness, or being bold—and most importantly, we are in a hurry. We don't have 2.5 hours to worry about washing clothes.

After my clothes were washed, I was told to take the clothes to a drying room. I asked for the key to the drying room, and inside this room, it was completely empty except for some wires running the length of the ceiling. I thought, *What are those for?* Eventually, I realized I should hang up my clothes to dry on the lines in the drying room, which took about two days to dry.

Tips. September of 1993. The USA is very service oriented, and servers receive a tip based on the service they provide. This does not exist in central Europe, in post-communist countries. They do not have a service-oriented perspective. In fact, many times, they do not care whether you buy something or not when you go in the store. At that time, most of the stores were still owned by the government, or some "cooperative," so unless it was an unusual person, most of the workers were not that motivated. Tips were considered strange, and maybe an attempt to bribe someone; however, tips are becoming more normal, and now a tip is when you round the bill up to the next dollar. However, this is also changing, and in many places, you need to ask what the custom is for tipping.

Mothers. This part of central Europe, especially in the Czech Republic, allows a parent to have their salary during the first two years of being home with a newborn. (Of course, you pay nothing for the birth of the child.) And the next two years, there is a decrease in the money, but the previous job must be waiting when they return. And if they are pregnant again, it starts over. There are also many "mother's schools," a place to leave your child if you want for a brief time while you are doing some errands.

Outside of the town of Olomouc is this beautiful church on a hill. After one of the visions of Mary, the church was built in memory of this occasion. It has become a pilgrim site and a local place for weddings.

Shoes. No shoes inside homes, especially ones you were wearing outside. The idea is that the soles of your shoes carry all sorts of germs, bacteria, and viruses, so basically, you take your shoes off at the door and put on slippers, which they will have there at the door. Of course, there are exceptions to this, but I thought it allowed for some very funny situations when someone had some shoes matching their outfit and ended up putting on another person's slippers to wear in the house. And, in some formal situations, where evening clothes were worn to a nice event, I saw people changing out of their outdoor shoes into nicer indoor shoes.

The big holiday of Easter Monday. For many people in central Europe, Easter is an important holiday, and Sunday is the traditional observance of church traditions. However, Monday is Easter Monday. This is some type of leftover tradition of the rite of spring, some Celtic rituals, something to do with fertility and eggs. It differs slightly from village to village, but often the boys and men spend time with women who are important to them (usually sisters, wife, mothers, aunts, and possibly some friends). They sit, talk, eat something, and then they go through the local ritual of gently hitting the woman on the leg or rear with a special rod with ribbons, cut from a special tree (usually father and son go and do this); in return he gets an egg, and maybe a drink of slivovica (homemade brandy). This happens with any woman who is important to you. She is patiently, silently, waiting for you at her home. I was told (with a wink and a nod), "You must understand, we need this. We need to be hit so we can continue to be alive and active." Other women I also knew were so disgusted with this old tradition, they would leave the country! (Easter Monday seemed to be celebrated more in the Czech Republic than in Croatia.)

Atheism in the Czech Republic. Sometimes, at Christmas or Easter, I would talk about American holidays, and I would share about my faith and why I am a believer. After my class, one girl came to me and said, "Donald, you must understand that we are proud to be atheists." Historically, there were some difficult situations with the Catholic Church in this part of the world, and there was some confusion about the Thirty

Years' Religious War in this part of Europe, so I think they really meant to say, "We are spiritual folks, open-minded to religion and its various ideas, but we do not want to be part of the traditional church." Yet, I met many Czech Catholics, and in Olomouc, at the St. Mary of the Snow Church was a weekly gathering of students with about five hundred attending. And adding to the confusion, most of the Czech churches were full! In surprising contrast, Croatia is traditionally Catholic, and even the atheists in Croatia would claim to be Catholic.

Car and drive school for children. In almost every town, often located near a park, there would be an area dedicated to teaching children about the skills of driving. They could ride bikes, walk, or rent something like a slow toy car, and they would "pretend" to drive in this area. There were little hills, sidewalks, stop signs, walking paths, and circular turns. There would be lights that change in the right way. It could be fun, or there may be an entire classroom of students showing up to learn the basics of driving safety in a small safe way. (Interestingly, however, for me, driving in central Europe was not nice—very impatient drivers, forcing you to move over so they can overtake you, and people seemingly driving with a bad attitude, rather than a cooperative one.)

Every town has a swimming pool. These are large pools that are indoors and heated. There is usually a very fun slide that can be several stories tall. When you go to the changing room, there is a line on the floor where your outdoor shoes are not allowed. You must take them off and go barefoot or bring some slippers to wear. Also, the typical large bathing suits (that many men in the USA wear) are not allowed. They want single-layer, small bathing suits, similar to what you see on swimmers that are used in competition. If you don't have one of these, they have them for sale! Also, every swimming pool has a sauna, wet and dry, and in the summertime, the large indoor pool is open to the outside. The fee for the pool is based on the amount of time you spend in the pool area.

Walking streets in downtown areas. Most of the towns in Europe have a center of the town where there are no cars, or if they are allowed, it is only for parking. These walking areas create a wider space in the center of town, often around various beautiful buildings. There will be cafés and chairs for sitting, fountains, and gardens in these areas.

Winter and summer tires. In northern Europe, you must have two sets of tires. When the temperature reaches a certain level, then you must change your tires. So, you can imagine, you don't just have a set of tires on your car; you also have another four tires sitting in your garage waiting to be changed according to the season. If you miss the date, you can be fined. The winter tires have small metal "hooks" to hold them on the snow or ice. You can leave your winter tires on all the time if you choose. Usually at the designated time (after an official announcement), you see people everywhere changing their tires or taking them to a tire place. (This was completely true in the Czech Republic, not in Croatia.)

Train system and train stations. There is an extensive train system in Europe. Some of the largest buildings, even in small towns, are these train stations. And many times, the trains are full. So the train station is like a small village all of its own with shops, and it's very busy. You soon learn what to do, which platform to stand on, and where to sit. If it is a busy time, careful folks will reserve a seat, but most times it is not necessary, yet on Fridays, Sundays, or holidays, you should reserve a seat. Interestingly, there aren't many school buses for children. The public transport is so extensive, and they simply take the public transport to their school. Usually, next to the train station is also a bus station, taking one to places the train could not reach. If the train was not going to a certain village, then the bus was for sure. In Croatia, I would see many students at the bus station sending their clothes home to mother in some remote village to be washed. They would come and pick up clean, neatly folded clothes from the bus the next day! The bus driver usually knew the family.

*There are two clock towers in the Czech Republic: one is in Prague,
and the other is in Olomouc. Prague's has retained its Biblical and
Catholic symbols; however, in Olomouc, where the Russian army
headquarters had set up camp, they decided to throw away the
religious symbols and create their own socialist perspective of time.*

Overtaking. People drive close behind you and want you to move over so they can overtake you. They want you to drive on the very right side of the road, so they can pass. This has happened to me, even when an approaching car on the other side is coming; they just slide in between. Then I started noticing that people do this also while walking, biking, and snow skiing. This is hard to get used to; in my country, we are taught to stay way behind. But beware in both areas, if the person behind you runs into you, it is always their fault. And when someone would overtake me, I would often be surprised at the interesting looks everyone would give me as they went by. I would smile and wave at them.

Socialist mindset. Perhaps due to forty years of communism, folks in this area of the world are much more social-minded toward others. Or they don't mind tax money going to help those in need, or for medicine, or to build parks, bicycle paths, walking paths, or housing for those in need. Further, public transport is very extensive, and the entire scope of medicine is not for business; it is rather a service for the public, dedicated to keeping the population healthy. However, a lot of this has changed since 1990, and more and more countries have incorporated some sort of insurance for medicine. Education through the university level is also paid for by the state. All of these expenses are taken from the salary of the individual as well as social security or retirement. During the communist regime, everyone worked, no one stayed at home, and each person's work was their own contribution to the welfare of everyone. This carried over, and today almost everyone works in these countries.

Hard to explain. Most people in this part of central Europe lived in a block of flats with others, had very similar flats, and shared a common yard downstairs. Most everyone seemed to be in a similar financial situation. Yet, it's hard to explain, one may come across something like this home pictured nearby. A beautiful private home, newly built, with expensive landscaping and architecture. Most likely this family was able

This is a single-family dwelling near Olomouc. Note the tile roofs, which are common with homes like this, the extensive flower garden, and fencing.

to gain some additional money after 1990, perhaps from a private business, but as I said, it's hard to explain.

Zoos. Almost every town with a population of one hundred thousand or more also had a zoo. The one in Olomouc was a great place to visit and take friends. Also, each zoo has a different "popular" animal. For example, the one in Olomouc had a special herd of giraffes. In another town one hour away, the special animal was a large ape.

Unfriendly to strangers. If you don't know someone, you do not speak or even look at them. Rather, they are part of your daily problem, and those people you don't know need to get out of the way. Rarely did I ever have a stranger look me in the eye, and say, "Good morning," or "Dobrý den," or "Ahoj." One time at a ski area in Moravia, I was being friendly and just spoke to a lady, and her reply (in English) was, "I do not know you!" And in contrast, if you know someone, or are lucky enough to make a friend there, they feel very close to you, and you are like family, sleeping and eating in their homes. I assume all of this may be due to the time of the Nazis or communism when one did not know who to trust.

Recreation. People in this area are involved with gardening, cultural events, weekend houses, pubs, and mushrooming, and on Thursday, they will ask you, "What is your plan for the weekend?" The adults are very busy working Monday through Friday; the communist influence instilled a social perspective that everyone contributes and is working. Therefore, the weekend is very important. I would be amazed at the detailed plans people would have, especially for walking, or mushrooming, or bicycling through the countryside. They would have various stops outlined, and in many of these remote places hidden in some forest, there would be a café or pub to stop and relax or maybe sleep. I learned about a part of their history, something called "tramping," where groups of folks would meander across forests and stay in the woods. Many people also had garden plots, in large areas with others, with cute little huts built, even weekend houses; small huts where everyone could sleep. This is fairly easy to do because the government had seized all of the property in the 1950s, and the population was welcome to go meandering in the woods and forests.

Mushrooming. This is an old tradition in this area, going into the forest to find healthy fungi to preserve and eat. Often done with grandpa, or other family, maybe friends, it's an idyllic pastime shared with memories and intense focus on doing something healthy. I joined one friend's father, and he took me on a three- to four-hour adventure of crawling and hiking through the Jesenick woods to find his favorites. After we returned home, every available table was full of these mushrooms. He cleaned them, turned them over carefully, and looked at and studied them, and they began to preserve them for use during the winter. One of the best soups I have ever had was mushrooms from the forest and potato soup. There is a wonderful culture here of mushrooming, and it is carefully taught, sometimes in the schools. It is all about nature, healthy living, and positive leisure time.

My friend Mirek with the mushrooms we had gathered.

The local pub. Almost every neighborhood in the Czech Republic had a local "hospoda," or pub. This is a very friendly place, almost like your den at home. There would be a small area, or bar, with seats and there you could order. There would be an assortment of "pub food" (such as sausage and bread) and then a list of pivo (beer) that would be offered that day. Instead of staying at home, many folks come with children and dogs to the local pub. They share a drink and their stories of the day, and it's really a lovely idea. There may be some folks in a corner playing a card or board game. Others may be talking seriously, but in general, it was an open atmosphere, welcome to anyone, and a very friendly place. Although overindulgence in alcohol is not tolerated, having a drink is very much a normal part of daily life, especially homemade brandies and wine. In my favorite pub in Olomouc, U Kuděje, sometimes, someone would pull out a guitar and people would start singing. I would estimate there was room for forty. In the summer, people would sit outside and enjoy the evening.

Chapter Seventeen:

Travel Is a School

Scenario. March of 1994. The first year in Zagreb, several of us joined our neighbors on a whirlwind trip through Croatia. Over Easter, there were going to be several days off, so I had asked our neighbors, who were Croatian (Tony and Gordina) if we could hire them to take five of us to see their famous coast. I will always remember the view of the Adriatic from the top of the Velebit mountains. Shockingly beautiful turquoise water, with islands scattered across the horizon as if some giant had skipped a thousand stones and they all stayed. When we approached the old town of Zadar, there was a "floating bridge." Tony said, "Don't worry, the Serbs have shot down our other bridge, but this one is okay, as long as there is no shooting today."

Travel Is a School: Some Thoughts and Ideas

Travel can be a way to live your dreams in our world. Well, that is for those who like to venture outside of their home. One travel writer Chris Pearce has described the experience of travel as similar to a ladder. Perhaps stretching some of his ideas and combining them with Maslow's Hierarchy of Needs, one can say the first step on the ladder is a comfortable travel experience. Perhaps something close to home or the typical one-week vacation with your parents. The next step would maybe be a school or church group, with friends and counselors or chaperones. So, travel is like climbing a ladder; each rung in the ladder is the way to make and mold you into an independent and caring traveler. Next, could be a trip with some friends, unsupervised. Then joining tour groups, hiring tour guides, buying insurance, on and on, until you become more comfortable and arrive at the top as the independent and satisfied self-planned traveler. Mezirow introduced the idea of change, even transformation, as a result of difficulty or conflict. This can take place in travel, and possibly resulting in Maslow's "peak experiences" during certain travel situations.

Planning a trip. Planning a trip today is not a problem. First, for trips outside of the USA, make sure you have a passport that is current (this can take six months to receive). Second, go to a travel agent, and they can organize for you almost anything. When you want to be more independent, you can use travel books (go to a bookstore and ask for travel books or purchase them online), the internet (go to your search engine and type in where you want to go), or ask others. Also, on YouTube, you can find examples of travel trips to almost any place on the globe. And now, with the advent of advertising on YouTube, motivated and creative travelers are trying to get a following through their unique and special trips. Just go to YouTube, type in "travel to _____" (where you are going), and see what comes up. Then you can organize the entire trip yourself over the internet, from the air ticket to the train rides to the hotels. Even popular museums can be reserved ahead of time. So, it's simple really—if you are connected to the internet ("world wide web" as we used to say) and are comfortable using it.

If for some reason you cannot do this, go to your local library and ask for some internet help, or find a high school or college student and pay them to help you. For others, using a travel agent, or talking to someone who has gone, can also be the best solution. Where I live now, in South Georgia, I have been surprised by the number of group trips being offered especially for seniors. For example, one bank in this community offered a ten-day trip to see Pennsylvania. All of it by bus, driving to various hotels, and seeing lots of great places along the way. So, join them for their trip, keep your journal of places to stay and good choices, and then return the next year and take who you want. Another opportunity is Road Scholar (formerly Elderhostel), which offers education-oriented travel everywhere. These interesting trips with a learning angle cover every type of travel, plus you are going with a group that easily mingles and interacts with one another.

I want to add that a trip to "anywhere" can also be very simple, safe, and easy. I recommend going to a popular destination, such as Rome, Paris, Amsterdam, or London. Reserve a room in a reputable hotel for one week and simply stay there and make it your home for a week. Then the people in the hotel can help you to discover what you want to see. A trip like this allows you to relax, to come back to the same room each day, and to get to know the area around your hotel. In each of the places I listed, you can find very interesting things to do every day. So if you do something like this, I recommend staying in at least two of these large cities. The easiest way is to fly into London, stay in the center for three to five days, and then take the Eurostar to Paris, and do the same there, then fly home out of Paris.

Embracing trends in travel. And, for the independent traveler, there are always new ways to go, such as Airbnb, different types of "house exchange," Road Scholar, CouchSurfing, or Vrbo. Many folks have been inspired by the Airbnb rage, and they have fixed up abandoned rooms, attics, and barns, so you can stay in a lot of unique places. If you are young, or very bold, try the couch surfing experience. Europe has been offering rooms in homes for years; "pension" is the usual name. When you are driving on some of the rural back roads of beautiful old Europe, you will see a sign saying, "pension" at a home. Stop in and ask for the price. It often includes a breakfast, but you will be staying inside someone's home, and likely sharing a bathroom. I highly recommend it.

Great trips can be easily had if you plan and be flexible, take easy-to-handle luggage, take less rather than more, journal your activities and experiences, meet locals, and continue to learn when you return. For example, when you come back from that trip to Rome, go to the library and find a book on Rome and continue to learn. I usually take clothes for a week, and then I will find somewhere to do laundry. Wear lots of polyester blends and black; it travels well and rarely shows dirt. Another trick I have used is to take all of my old clothes, and instead of giving them to Goodwill, I use them on the trip, and closer to the end of the journey, I leave them on park benches, put them in a clothes recycling bin, or just throw them away. Probably the most important is a good pair of broken-in shoes!

Traveling alone. Well, my friend, get over it. Often the older we get, the more alone we are. I know of hundreds of people who are so frustrated because they cannot get their husband, wife, or whoever, to travel with them where they want to go. I want to invoke the memory of two ladies. One a seventeen-year-old and the other an eighty-year-old. Both of whom I met on trains in Europe, and both of whom were traveling completely alone. The seventeen-year-old from Australia was traveling the globe for a year. And the eighty-year-old, who was walking on the paths of Switzerland, was traveling after becoming widowed. They both inspired me with their lack of fear, their willingness to continue to travel alone, and their zest for life. They were very brief encounters with both of them, yet both impacted me. I was sitting on a train, riding through the Bavarian part of Germany. Previously the car (on the train) had been full, but now it was just this young lady and I; we made eye contact, and I said hello. I asked her about her trip when I realized she was not a local. "I left Australia about six months ago, and I am wandering around the globe, no set agenda, just enjoying each day, and each place." I was struck by her confidence and calmness. During this time, I was trying to decide whether I could handle living in another country for a year. Inside I was thinking, *Listen, Donny, if this young lady, who is alone, can live away from her family, friends, and culture for a year, certainly you can.* The other woman I met in the Bernese Oberland. I was in the high mountains of Switzerland on one of the small trains that cross the mountains, and this older lady and I nodded at each other and began a conversation. I cannot remember the details of this lady's life, except for this part: "Well, I love to travel, and now I can. You see, I recently became widowed, buried my husband, so now I refuse to stay in that situation. I decided I would travel, and I am thoroughly enjoying it." She was also so calm, and at peace, as she got off the train and started on one of the trails. Again, inside this tutor from the "school of travel" is telling me, *Look, Donny, here is someone much older than you, who is doing these interesting and daring travel adventures.* I decided then that I would go for the one-year program of living in Croatia.

I recommend, whatever your situation, that you make a list of where you want to travel in your life and begin to make plans and go there. If others join you, then great, but do not depend on others to go; you can travel alone. As discussed earlier, the number one reason why people choose not to do something is because they say, "I don't have anyone to go with me. I can't do this on my own." I invite you to change this perspective. Further, the more people you invite or hope to join, each one will have their own special problem or issue. There are some rare situations where entire families may be able to join, but usually not, or something will change someone's plans. So, take control of this important aspect of your life and make a list. For example, I am going to start with a long dreamed of trip to Egypt in three years. I will invite my favorite ten friends to join. And, if it happens that I am alone, then I will be prepared and take that book I have always wanted to read. It's okay to be alone, and I think that once you get used to it, you will see there is a new freedom involved. I think the highest level of travel is when you are alone, where you are free to meet others and to investigate those issues in your life that are presented. When you are traveling in a group, even with one other person, your focus is often on them, what they are thinking, how they are, and whether they are enjoying the trip. This is referred to as a shrinking of your world. When you travel with others, it's easy for your world to shrink to the folks that you are with. The more people you take, the more complicated this becomes. I have seen tour groups of twenty to thirty people, all from one country, stick together like a swarm of bees, trying to cross the Charles Bridge in Prague. They would be talking about their trip, or things about home, and would be oblivious to all that was going on around them.

Learning how to pack. The lighter you pack, the happier you will be. If you can imagine it, I recommend traveling with the barest minimum. This would include three to four pairs of underwear, easily washable T-shirts, and socks. Make sure your shoes are sturdy and comfortable and can be on your feet on a walking trail or at the theater. You will simply wash out the above-mentioned garments every fourth day and let them dry overnight. You will wear the rest of your clothes every day. I recommend a black pair of pants, polyester, and a black shirt. If you need more clothes, you can buy them, and they can be unique souvenirs.

Avoiding travel traps. Travelers have extra money. People usually do not go into debt to travel, and therefore, it is assumed that the traveler has disposable money, and most travelers would like a souvenir. Artful and well-planned souvenirs are interesting to see and may be a genuine object to bring home. If I was in Orlando, Florida, I would not mind buying some locally produced honey, but I am not interested in a T-shirt from Disney World made in Guatemala. The couple from South Georgia, whom I mentioned earlier, Bill and Nell, traveled maybe twenty-five times to Europe and never bought a souvenir. One trip, when I was in Israel for two months and I was able to see a lot of historic religious places, I was so surprised by the number of people spending so much time in the souvenir shops. They are walking through the aisles trying to find the perfect souvenir from their experience. Outside was the tomb of Lazarus and they were more interested in cheaply made objects in the souvenir shops than the actual site.

My friend, you won't find what you are looking for in that souvenir shop. The best souvenirs are drawings you make while looking at the Matterhorn, a small rock picked up and taken home, a picture, or just a journal entry. Try something different; take a recorder, or use your phone, and just record your day. I suggest that the best souvenir is a memory of talking with a local person and being with them. I can recall on one trip to Madrid, Spain, I was sitting in a McDonald's and just finishing a Big Mac. Next to me was a family, and I thought, *I have to say something.* So quietly, and distinctly, I asked them, "Excuse me, do you speak English?" and "Are you from here?" We had such a great thirty-minute conversation about life in Madrid, Spain, which was way beyond what any tour guide or information you find in a guidebook could tell you. If you must bring a souvenir, especially for grandkids, I recommend going into a local grocery store and finding some candy or salty snacks, something local that you cannot find at home, and bringing that home.

Realize that some people working in tourism are going to try to get more money from you, and maybe they deserve it. In restaurants, try to review your bill and leave a small tip. I would not buy an expensive item while on a trip. If you see something you like, take a picture, think about it, and buy something like it at home. My mom was carried away with small marble "eggs" she saw in Italy, which is famous for marble. They are beautiful, but my poor dad had to carry a bag of thirty-five marble eggs from Italy. It made a good joke for their traveling friends, and by the way, we still don't know what to do with those marble eggs. There are exceptions to everything, and if you find something you really like, then send it home the cheapest way possible. For example, when I was traveling in Bosnia, I came across one foundation making rugs; I decided I wanted something like this, and eventually I asked a friend whether they could bring it with them home to the USA. Today if you come to my house, you will walk on this rug. Eventually, I had most of the things I had accumulated shipped to the USA. At that time, you had two choices: put something on a ship and then it takes several weeks to reach you (should be nothing breakable), or pay for express delivery by airmail. This should only take a few days and is much more expensive. So, today when you are traveling and you find an irresistible souvenir, take it to the local post office, insure it, and ship it home—it should take almost three weeks.

Money. You need a reliable credit card that can work from anywhere, and you need to call your credit card company to tell them before you go. Also, you will need a reliable ATM in order to withdraw local money (you must also contact your bank and tell them know where you will be) and a passport. And then you want to practice withdrawing money and using the credit card in the USA before you go. Also, take some cash in a money belt, and practice wearing the money belt and accessing it. The cheapest way is to carry cash with you, and then you can exchange this for local currency at a reliable money exchange store. These topics are changing a lot, and right now you can use a Capital One card around the world with no service charges, for the money conversion. However, with other cards, it can be 10–20 percent! And with an ATM, the charges have increased a lot since I first traveled in 1993. That is why bringing cash is better than getting money from an ATM. Bank transfers are also possible.

All of this takes time and knowledge, so get this straightened out one or two months before you travel.

Passport. In order to travel, especially internationally, you need to get this straight because you must have the right documents, or you can be sent home. First is the passport. I always have a copy of it, and I keep the main document in my room. I normally leave it in my suitcase. If someone asks for it, I show the copy in my billfold, and if they demand the real passport, I will return to the hotel and get it. Some countries will accept a driver's license for identification. Most countries have a national identification card; the USA does not, but a driver's license may pass for this. But the passport you must have somewhere nearby.

Phone and internet. Check with your local phone service for international phone calls. You can also use a local SIM card and replace the one that's in your current phone. Facebook Messenger and WhatsApp also work everywhere in the world where there is Wi-Fi, and some phone services allow for texting. Email always works over the internet. This will take some energy and time to figure out. If you have people you *must* keep in touch with, then this will take some time and effort to understand. Also, you should practice it before you go. Keep in mind some countries are not as open about use of the internet as in the USA, try to check this before you leave.

Be prepared to wait. During travel, via bus, air, or train, there are delays—patience is the best way to enjoy travel. And be prepared to be delayed. Have something extra to do if you need to wait—an interesting book, crossword puzzle, etc.—something that will make your wait enjoyable. I always carry a Kindle book, phone, journal, and work-oriented information, and I somehow continue to work on all of these. For some people, these experiences, especially in a foreign country, cause a lot of stress. Keep in mind, stress is not all bad. Some stress is good, and it can even energize you to want to learn more. But too much stress is negative. I recommend leaving the comfort of your home, taking a risk, enjoying travel, and meeting a local, and your world will expand. You will understand the world better and feel more confident about life and travel.

It is a spiritual endeavor to go on a journey. The Bible is full of stories of travelers, as well as other religious books. The ancient writings really begin with the journey of the Jewish nation traveling from Egypt to Palestine. Abraham took his family on a journey to Palestine. And the writer Paul went on three journeys—Turkey, around the Mediterranean, and even Greece—proclaiming the good news. Travel is a step of faith mainly because you have to trust others, especially others you don't know—a pilot, a tour guide, the stranger sitting next to you. Always go to the internet and read what the USA State Department says about the area you are going to. If there is a warning about a certain country, stay away. Realize that the world is a friendly place, and most people will be happy to meet you, and merchants will try to please you in order to earn your money. Always ask politely, "Excuse me, do you speak English?" And if you are ready for high-level travel, when you are in a coffee shop, pub, or museum, reach out to someone and ask, "Excuse me, are you from here? Do you speak English? Can you tell me about your country?"

The Density of Travel

I was somewhere on an island in the Mediterranean. I met a man on the boat, or ferry. He and his wife were from the USA and were returning to their current location. "Oh yes, you see we just went to get the mail. See we are living here now, or rather we live on the road, traveling, and in a way, we will plan to be in some area about four to six months, and you can get your mail delivered to the general postal center for that town. We let those know who need to know where we are, and if they need to send us something, they address it to the town center . . . and have our name on it . . . and it comes."

I was also on a trip. Not only was I living in central Europe, but I was currently on a vacation in Greece, and I was somewhat impressed with my own idea of travel until I met this man. This man had sold everything, given up everything, and simply lived around the world traveling with his wife. They are enjoying this new life while traveling around the globe in their recreational vehicle. And almost everywhere I have been, if you uncover enough of the folks around you, there is usually a type of permanent traveler. All sorts of younger generations wandering the globe and working their way around its firmament. At times I would meet folks who literally spend their life traveling. (This is in sharp contrast to how I was raised, where the only trip we ever made was the once-a-year, six-day trip to Daytona Beach, Florida.)

In the area I lived in in Olomouc, Czech Republic, I came across a middle-aged American man who was wandering the world. He was using the travel site CouchSurfing in order to make it as cheap as possible. There was a CouchSurfing social in the town, and this man happened to be there, and he told me his story. I began to wonder about the number of people around the world who are doing something similar, how often are they going, where are they staying, and how it is working out. Around the same time, I found a former student of mine who had decided to ride a bicycle around the world, and he was chronicling everything on a Facebook page. I would at times text him and he told me that there were many more who were also doing the same.

This type of traveler would most likely scoff at the thoughts inside this book. These folks often avoid hotels, or high-end travel ventures, preferring to explore the world in a more natural way, close to the folks who live there. But I wanted to acknowledge them since this is a travel book and to let them know that I am aware of their interesting life.

While living in the Czech Republic, I became friends with Mitch and Marie. These world travelers are living this philosophy. They often travel without an agenda and often decide where to go in a spontaneous way. They eat local food, avoid tourist areas, and are eager to meet local folks. They usually rent a car and enjoy exploring and discovering the country where they are traveling. They try to lay aside conventional information and warnings of various places and get to know places on their own.

Overcrowded situations of travel create some uncomfortable situations. After arriving at one's sought-out destination, the sojourner does not want to have to push, shove, and use one's shoulder in order to arrive at the place. I will never forget once when walking across the Charles Bridge in Prague, it became almost dangerous. Wall-to-wall folks, large travel groups huddling together, languages from around the world all descending on this ancient bridge for the folks to go from one part of Prague to the other without taking a ferry. Other situations lessen the authentic tourist experience. On one trip to Rome, there had descended on this part of Italy so many refugees selling Chinese-made plastic objects that you could not make it to the Spanish Steps without dodging these plastic flying objects that glowed at night. And the sadness of watching refugees out of place at the Eiffel Tower placing miniature Eiffel Towers on tattered blankets while the real object towered overhead, all resulted in a scene of divine comedy and sadness.

Other travelers simply create their own agendas and stay away from such scenes. They are looking for the authentic; they are bypassing all that smells of tourism and looking for the real. These folks are travelers but rarely would you find them in the world of tourism. They are hoping to stay with local people, or to meet them, eat local food, and avoid souvenir shops, and they do not have much of an agenda for travel. They can be very spontaneous, or simply ask others around them what to do. They try to put aside prejudice or things they have heard on the news and try to engage with the local people.

This results in sustainable travel or a more friendly way to be a tourist. Sustainable travel involves minimizing environmental impact, supporting local communities, and making eco-friendly choices while exploring destinations. Consider using public transportation, staying in eco-friendly accommodations, and respecting local cultures to promote sustainable practices.

My colleague from the Czech Republic, Miroslav Rončák, suggests that tourists must become more aware of their behavior and their choices. The players in this interesting scenario of tourism include local residents, owners of the actual tourist property, the site of the destination, and the tourist (at least). A coordinated effort to communicate with all four elements is essential. This is the heart of "good" tourism, or sustainable tourism, and prevents "overtourism." For example, in Prague, they are trying to coordinate this dialogue among these groups along the Royal Way. You perhaps have been there and walked the often-crowded Charles Bridge and then up to the castle. Now there are eight million tourists a year in Prague, and this dialogue has become necessary so that future generations can also enjoy Prague.

This respectful travel entails appreciating and embracing local customs, traditions, and people. It involves being mindful of cultural differences, practicing responsible tourism, and leaving a positive impact on the places you visit. This helps to avoid what some are calling overtourism, which is the excessive and unsustainable influx of tourists to a destination, causing negative impacts on the environment, local communities, and cultural heritage. It often leads to overcrowding, environmental degradation, increased living costs for locals, and a loss of the destination's authenticity. Places where there is significant beauty or wonder require an aggressive perspective of sustaining practice in order to avoid the negative issues of overtourism.

Chapter Eighteen:

Contrasts between the USA and Central Europe

S cenario. June of 1996. I had noticed the sign but kept going, not knowing what it meant. It was a beautiful rocky beach with unique coves, the typical clean turquoise water on the Adriatic. But interestingly I began to notice that the farther I went, the less clothing I saw. I was already used to seeing ladies without tops on the beach, but pretty soon, no one had any clothes. I knew I was out of place and, not sure what to do, I returned. There was someone at the entrance, very friendly, and a great English speaker. She said, "We are very proud here. We have almost thirty-five nudist beaches (called FKK) on the Croatian coast. They are scattered across the coastline. You Americans are so funny; you think this is about sex or having sex. You are so wrong. This is all about expression, freedom. It's a way of life. It's about the return to the way we used to live. There are probably more families here than single folks." (Question to reader, did I stay or leave?)

Study hall. Usually one travels with a suitcase. But each of us also carries individual invisible suitcases. These are filled with our own ideas, prejudices, anger, fears, and worries. Simply watch the behavior of others when you travel. It becomes obvious what is in the invisible suitcase. This type of "baggage'" can help or hurt my time during travel. In this chapter I present some of my baggage.

Photograph of the Auschwitz concentration camp of the Nazi regime, in southern Poland. Central Europe had a large Jewish population, so the signs of the previous Nazi influence were everywhere.

Earlier in my life, I thought that everyone wanted to be an American. I had grown up also thinking that my country was the best and the way we did things was the right way. Many of us see other countries as inferior, and that the way we do things is the best. Isn't this somewhat natural? When I visit my neighbor, I wonder why are they doing "it" that way, when we do "it" this way. The longer I lived in another country, the more I saw the error in this.

Although people in the USA look very similar to people in central Europe, we do almost everything differently. Each particular situation was interesting and a point in learning. For example, in that part of the world, for every meal, there is always a hot clear broth soup at the beginning of the meal—summer, winter, every meal—with rice, noodles, or mushrooms. They are convinced it prepares your stomach for food.

Many conservative Americans seem to think of Europe as liberal; rather, I saw a very conservative family-oriented society. Interestingly, Americans call themselves family oriented, yet they rarely would share a home with a sibling or a parent. We think each family must have their own kitchen! In the European mindset, they are willing to make room for all members of the family until they can be on their own. The grandparents are very involved in the family, and they are often the ones picking up grandchildren from school. There are rarely babysitters, as we know it in the USA; it has to be grandma or no one. Many families live together, or next to each other, and some homes are built on various floors, where one family will take one floor, and another one the other. Families do not split up; they stay and support each other. For example, in my family, I have relatives scattered a thousand miles across the eastern part of the USA, but this is very rare in central Europe. However, a lot of this is changing.

In the USA, sports are an integral part of the school system. Coaches, teams, cheerleaders, stadiums, concessions, and bands are normal in most schools, especially middle and high school. Some high schools in the USA have large stadiums and gymnasiums where sporting events are attended by thousands. However, in Europe, school is for learning, and physical education is part of the school activity. Sport usually takes place outside of the school system, and it is often aligned with the professional teams of that area. Fans rarely attend these local sporting events, except maybe parents or family members.

Most people over the age of sixteen drive in the USA. However, most of Europe is dependent on an effective public transport system that reaches into every corner of one's precinct. You can rely on the bus or train, and it is fairly on time. There will often be one car within one family in this area of Europe. There are not designated school buses in Europe because the students simply take the already-in-place public transportation. If one wants to drive, one must attend auto school, which is a private education focused on driving and costs about $1,000. After paying the fee and passing the test, you have a license to drive.

Americans feel comfortable, so they often tell everyone everything about their personal life, even folks they're meeting for the first time. They are often smiling, laughing a lot, and talking very loudly. The folks in central Europe would never tell anyone anything personal about their life, especially a stranger. In fact, most would never talk to a stranger, but rather look at them suspiciously.

Many Americans think that most of the world speaks, or should speak, English. The USA is a large country, and it is easy to live one's life and never hear another language. So in a group of people from mixed countries, it is often the best English speakers who dominate. This is probably because others are more insecure about how they may sound. Americans often misunderstand the verbal mistakes locals make. And the locals are very self-conscious of others listening to them speaking English. Knowledge of English, at this time, is a key to many doors opening in one's life. Eventually, I realized that most people who were interested in me really just wanted to speak with a native English speaker and practice their English. One of the most important ways to get around a particular country is to learn a few of their words. Language is a personal reflection of country and family.

These extra, hidden issues are often brought with us. The idea that my country is the best, or that the way we do things is right, can always interfere in relating to another person during travel. Try to listen to their way of life and how they are living life. In general, the USA may be too dependent on lawsuits, or a sense of fear, or overdependent on insurance or guns to feel safe. Conversations I have heard in the USA have included "Well, you need to buy this extra insurance on this product because you just don't know what will happen," "You need to have travel insurance because you just are not sure what may happen when you are traveling," "I need to have a gun in the house. We just feel safer, and you just don't know what will happen," "Well, I would recommend this extra insurance because if someone comes to your house, and if there is an accident, well, they may sue," "No, we cannot approve this program with students because what if someone gets hurt, or someone gets lost? A parent may sue us." This type of mentality does not exist outside of the USA. How ironic that in our country where we have everything, we are the most scared, the most stressed.

Chapter Nineteen:
Working in the Czech Republic

S cenario. November of 1997. We spent some time in an area of Bosnia, near the town of Tuzla. The Yugoslav Wars still lingered on in some of these areas. We were having seminars for teaching English, meeting students, and showing a movie about Jesus. Someone had arranged for us to stay with a couple from a church they were associated with. She was so happy to have us there, although they could not speak English. As I walked into her "flat," I was surprised at these large barrels of water, chest high to me. The translator smiled and said, "We have to save and store water in case of an emergency." This very sweet and kind lady made sandwiches for us when we left, with some sort of sandwich meat and butter. (Mayonnaise was expensive.) As I was eating this on the bus, I thought about how this woman cared for us so much, to make us her version of a sandwich, and she lived on so little. On our

way through that part of Bosnia, occasionally there would be a United
Nations army tank with its gun pointed directly at the road.

This is a partial view of the cathedral in Olomouc—St. Wenceslas.
It is a complex building with significant history in the Czech Republic
and was even a royal residence.

Special Class at Our School of Travel and Transportation–My Car Is Replaced by a Tram

In 1993 and 1994, I joined a group of recent graduates (although I was a
good twenty years older), and we were assigned to live in Zagreb, Croatia, to
work with a Christian student program (I have referred to this earlier). When
we arrived in Zagreb, we realized that the town had a network of public
transportation. The main transport was a tram. This tram ran on tracks, and
was electric, with something sticking out of the top to a live electrical wire.
It would stop about every four hundred yards, several minutes would pass
between stops on the tram, each one covering about one-third of a mile. You

needed a ticket to ride the tram, and you needed to buy this before boarding. If you did not have a ticket and someone asked you for it, then you could be fined. This happened to me several times. People from countries with public transport understand all of this, but, as Americans, we did not.

The trams are an integral part of the city life in central Europe.
I called it my Olomouc car, and I would ride it every day.
Here are my mom and brother on a visit. They look right at home!

Eventually, I started buying tickets for one month. This waiting, this riding together with strangers was a new experience for all of us. Having to ride a predetermined route with others, eventually we all started to appreciate and enjoy it. We would be shocked at times by how crowded the tram was, and how packed in the people were, pressed right into each other! It was a great lesson on being with others.

Every once in a while, there would be an interesting disturbance on the tram, maybe a Roma child would be begging, or a Roma band would walk through the crowded tram and play this enticing music and ask for money, or there would be a problem with someone's ticket, or maybe just a fight between passengers. If someone needs a seat (e.g., pregnant women, children, disabled people, older people) you are supposed to get up and offer your seat. This allowed for some funny situations. Sometimes I would get on the tram, and then one rider would look at me and offer me their seat. I thought, *This must be a very bad day.* And then I would have fun with this; I would see someone definitely younger than me, and I would get up and offer my seat to them, and they would run past shaking their head.

This woman is making a traditional Bosnian rug. Possibly a refugee and widow from the massacre at Srebrenica, she was doing this work at a United Nations Relief Center for women who had lost their families at Srebrenica. You can buy rugs online from them, from an organization called BosFam, Tuzla, Bosnia and Herzegovina. There are several in my house.

All of us had cars in the USA, so we were used to getting into our own car, alone, and driving wherever. And some of us even had garages at our homes, where you never had to walk out in the weather. We were used to making the car comfortable for us, with music, food, or airflow. In addition, you are surrounded by two thousand pounds of weight in a car, and therefore, it gives you a sort of feeling of invincibility. Whereas on the tram, it was about coming together with those in your area, making room, finding a safe place to stand or sit, and waiting for someone else to drive. Eventually, we all became comfortable with the tram system and enjoyed it.

Overall, this was a great lesson in life to learn to let go of the individual car and all of its conveniences and join the crowd inside a tram. How much better for the environment, this electric tram, where you don't have to worry about parking, and in fact, you don't have to worry about driving. You just sit down, or ride the tram, absorbed in your own thoughts, or maybe you are with a friend, and you just relax and leave the driving to the tram driver. Instead of being isolated while in a car, on the tram, you are surrounded by people, this humanity of others who are always wanting to get somewhere. You learn to wait, observe others, share, and be considerate of others.

I was raised to speak to strangers, to look them in the eye, with a smile and a handshake, and to say, "How are you?" In contrast, on the trams, if you don't know someone, you look quickly away, or look down, or now, look at your phone. With all the problems in this part of the world, I think the tram is the perfect place to bring people together. It is the custom here to speak to someone if you have previously met them. But it is not the custom to speak to a stranger. However, many times I would look at someone in the eye on the tram and nod my head in hello. I had many interesting responses.

Scenario. Fall of 2009. Soccer or "fudbal" is the most popular sporting activity in the world. Also, each team has its own fan club. And, within each fan club, there are certain elements that are extreme—these may be called "hooligans." If Zagreb was playing someone in fudbal, you could tell a difference in the city; police were lined up everywhere, and folks would tell me to watch out. One time in Olomouc, I joined a friend at a soccer match, and for some reason, the tickets we had were in this fan club section. We had to walk through police who were checking us for anything dangerous and then we sat in an area that was completely fenced in. It was like we were animals in a cage. We could not get out, and no one could get in. On the other side of the field was the other team's fan club, with the same setup. Often those sitting in opposite fan areas would be jeering at one another, screaming, making crude remarks, or crude symbols. The visitor fan club was escorted by the police from the train station to this fenced-in area, and then escorted back after the match. There was no chance for interaction with anyone. Often the hooligans of opposing teams would spend their time during the game trying to do something to get the other hooligans upset. It was as if two completely different contests were occurring: the one on the field, and then the one between fan clubs. I wondered to myself why are these young men being so violent and belligerent for a fudbal team? And more important I tried to understand how soccer, fudbal, could be the most played game in the world. I saw it everywhere. It is so simple, just kick a round object, back and forth. I have seen rolled-up trash used for a ball and rocks to make a goal.

This was taken several years ago as Croatia was playing for the World Cup in Fudbal or soccer. The game seems to create its own culture of sport as well as hooligans willing to fight for their team.

School Seminar on Working in Other Cultures: Working in Croatia and the Czech Republic

I originally worked in Zagreb with a USA-based Christian organization. Therefore, I was not really part of the Croatian work system. I worked for an American company and my assignment was based in Croatia. In order to stay any length of time like this, you must have a certain type of visa, so we obtained a language learning visa, as we were trying to learn to speak some of the Croatian language.

When I returned in 2004, I tried my chances at a tourist visa. I could stay in Croatia for three months, leave the country, and then have my passport stamped again, and that was good for three more months. But this was not the intention of the tourist visa, and eventually, I felt I needed to leave if I could not get a regular job. I did some work with the organization Udruga Fokus (this was the group I was with in '93, '94, '96, and 97), and I was able to give some lectures to different colleges in the area. I was also involved in research on the topics of exercise, walking, and tourism. These were all eventually published in academic journals.

One Czech university had expressed interest in me, and I decided to try to make it work. I would have to leave Croatia, after eight years, and all of the friends and connections I had there. However, I was thrilled that this Faculty of Physical Culture, which is part of Palacký University, wanted to hire me. They wanted a native English speaker. I would be teaching classes in research and recreation, and I would mainly be a part of their Erasmus program. I would be given a regular work visa and pay taxes to the Czech government and have the right to use their medical system.

The highest salary I had varied from $800 to $1,200 a month depending on different situations. It was an unusual situation to have someone working at the university on a full-time basis who was not Czech, and also not a part of the European Union. It became a lot of paperwork to get the necessary work visas as well as periodic visits with the international police.

Here is a typical large farmhouse in the Alps area of Europe.
Usually the family stays in the front area, the rooms upstairs are for tourists,
and the back of the house turns into a barn and houses all of the livestock.

Scenario. Summer of 1995. I took a bus from the train station to a village in the Swiss Alps to meet my friends that I met the previous year at a youth hostel. None of us were "youths," but we were staying there. This couple, Manfred and Regula, were maybe the most eco-friendly people I have ever known. When I visited them, they gave me the address, so I waited on the right bus and then began an adventure to the highlands of Switzerland. It was a classic Swiss village on a slanted hill, with a huge drop-off and a large lake at the bottom. I loved listening to them describe their way of life, their type of travel, and simply how they view the world. (He is a mechanical engineer and she is a schoolteacher.) After a few days, it was time for me to leave, Manfred offered me a ride in his "sun" car. It looked like one of those really narrow race cars. Every time you put on brakes down the mountain, it stores electricity for the return trip. Only pedals and brakes were inside this car. The two of us barely fit in this modern-era idea. I thought, *I have a lot to learn.*

Here is probably a retired couple returning from mushrooming in the forest—notice the baskets of mushrooms—and waiting on the tram in Olomouc, Czech Republic. These mushrooms will provide a hearty part of many meals during the upcoming cold winter.

Chapter Twenty:
Life in the Czech Republic

S cenario. September of 1996. We were in the region of Tuzla, Bosnia, contacting students, teaching English, and showing a movie about Jesus. This was a region with three distinct beliefs: Catholic, Ortho-dox Christian, and Muslim. During the Yugoslavia years, they reluctantly got along and put up with each other until the late 1980s and after the death of Tito. Eventually, the Yugoslav Wars affected each country as they tried to wrestle away from the dominance of Serbia. The Muslim influence within Bosnia is a very long and complicated history. It is so interesting to hear the call to prayer, notice the minarets on the skyline, see the different markers in cemeteries, and observe the style of clothes. Regardless, we were there to have some Christian influence. We showed this movie about Jesus, and we held an informal English workshop. After we showed a movie about Jesus, in some community center, there were also people we did not know handing out brochures to those who came. Someone locally told me, "Don't look at them, and don't bother them. They are Muslim and are offering a counter perspective of what you were presenting." This was okay for me. I did not mind them being there, even though it was maybe the first time I had ever seen someone countering the perspective I was presenting.

The Czech Republic has castles everywhere. This one, designated UNESCO, is in Litovel. Notice all of the interesting artwork created on the stucco.

The School of Travel offers a special tutor. This personal tutor will be with you during your time helping to guide and direct your learning.

Living versus Traveling

Because I was actually living in Zagreb, Croatia, and then in Olomouc, Czech Republic, rather than being a tourist, I could experience things much more deeply. No one pays much attention to tourists. They are traveling, so "What consequence is that? They are here and gone." I had already done the "here and gone" version of travel. I had seen some really amazing places, and so, I wanted to live there. I wanted to talk to the people, meet them for coffee at quaint cafés, eat with them in local restaurants, and go to church with them. Because of this, I was able to get to know people much more, folks like Branimir, Silvije, Mladen, Dasa, Mila, and Olinka. I met hundreds of folks and some of these folks became my friends, I could call them, meet them, and speak honestly with them. They took me to their homes, where I had meals with their families, and their grandmothers loved me and would sometimes greet me with a kiss on the lips!

I entered into the daily life of the Croat and then the Czech. I had been raised to be friendly, so I would knock on some of the doors in the buildings where I lived and say hello. In each area where I lived, on some holiday, I would invite neighbors to come and have a meal and get to know each other better. They were not used to that. These were formerly communist countries, and the regimes would usually create an atmosphere of distrust. Most of my neighbors had three or four locks on their doors!

Winter of 2007. I became involved in the cultural life of Europe— opera, symphony, ballet, concerts. I was able to enjoy and savor the old architecture of the beautiful buildings, usually built by kings or some local reigning person in charge, such as an archbishop within the Catholic Church. I thoroughly enjoyed the café life. Zagreb especially is well known for its café culture, and on Saturday morning to go for coffee in the center is amazing to see. Hundreds of cafés filled with people meeting and talking. One Croatian lady told me, "Donald, we do not need to go to a psychologist. We go to the pub, and there we discuss and talk about everything."

There was a movie culture about Zagreb, especially with the university students and younger folks. People loved movies, and afterward, they liked to go to a pub or café and have a discussion. The public transportation in these cities made transport around very easy. I like the inclusive aspect of the health care system. For them, health care is a right of each citizen.

When you live abroad, you must adapt and change your ways of living to their ways of living. You are a guest in their home or country, and you must be a responsible guest. This involves learning some of their language, learning about their culture, and supporting their country and its programs. Then when you return to where you are eventually going, you must pack up, end those living relations, or change them from living ones to visiting ones, and then you must change your way to the way of the world to which you are going. I am still doing this. It is not easy to know how to live in this way. I have lived in eight distinct places with their own communities, neighbors, and churches, and I have made great friends and left amazing people everywhere. "How to keep up relations with people who are important to you" is one of the main issues of life. But today it's easier than ever with the internet and mobile phones.

Scenario. One of the most interesting people I saw was a retired person, an older man, who was constantly getting in the way of the trams. At the main square of Zagreb, there was a crossing, for several trams. It was rather busy, and there were a lot of people getting on and getting off the trams. The tram would be approaching, and all of a sudden, this older man, with all of the swagger one could muster, all the authority that has been diverted into a head of state, would step boldly and unabashedly onto the tracks, as if he were the commander of the universe, motioning for the tram to come forward, or slow down, or stop. (Of course, it was easy to tell the tram was about to stop.) Then he would rush to the side and motion for the actual driver of the tram to open the door, which of course the driver did, and this man would sometimes even show the passengers the way to walk. Before the tram would begin, he would pretend to be the person in charge, telling the driver to prepare or to leave. I was taken in by this man's drama. How he created this world of make believe out of the silence and quiet of his own life. When you live in an area, you become more aware of the mental needs of folks, and sometimes in large cities, it is more evident, and sadly, we know this is a universal issue. The man was completely happy, full of energy, and purpose; I thought, *Hmmm, can I be so employed when I am an older man?*

Chapter Twenty-One:

Working in a Different Country

S cenario. The town of Split, Croatia, is a special place. This was the summer home of the ruthless Roman emperor, Diocletian. This port city is built around the remains of his large palace. The palace, built almost two thousand years ago, directly on the water, was a sprawling, large complex fit for an emperor. It is so large the city grew around it. Within the ancient walls of limestone, there are times when the heat in this area can be stifling. Although it is on the Adriatic, sometimes there is a hot, still air. Nothing moves, people dart from shadow to shadow, trying to find a place to sit. I was with one friend from this area. "Come, Donald, let's sit here, under the shade. We will have some coffee. This is a time, Donald, to just be quiet. Don't talk. It's the heat; it's the time we call 'Fiaka.' You see, all is okay. You don't need to move, or talk, or think, just be, and enjoy the coffee."

When I was a child, we were always scared of the principal, and the prevailing thought among all of us was that she had an electric paddle to keep us behaving well. In the school of travel, the principal can take different forms. But take heed, there is always a lesson to learn as well as a correction.

Confusion at Work

I was initially in Zagreb when I was working with an international USA-based Christian program, Campus Crusade for Christ (today called Cru). Later, when I returned to Zagreb in 2007, I had a PhD from the University of Georgia, and I had the ability to offer lectures in various colleges. I gave some volunteer lectures and some for pay in the areas of travel and tourism, sport, recreation, aging, and research. I spoke at various "schools" within the Zagreb University: the Medical College, the National Library, Business School, Philosophy College, School of Social Work, and the Sport College, and I would ask the professor what they would like me to speak about. These classes were one or two days and were fun oriented. The students had to listen to me speak in a foreign language to them, but most were supposed to know some level of English. This allowed me to get to know a lot of students, some I keep up with today. It was easy and fun, and it indicates the respect that most of the world has for the USA and the influence of the English language.

However, the "powers that be" were not willing for me to really enter into their academic world. I tried at the departments of social work, adult education, sport, and philosophy. My actual PhD is in adult education or lifelong learning, and I gave a few lectures there and really wanted them to hire me, but I could tell it just was not working out. They liked to talk to me in English about American politics, or life in the USA, or some movie or music they liked. Eventually, a professor in the adult education program said, "You have no place here."

Despite all of this, because I was American and spoke clear English, many people were very nice to me and would try to engage with me. And the students, especially, were very open and wanted to talk to me, just to see what this American was like. People had a positive view of our country, and they wanted to speak English with a native speaker. People also wanted me to hear their views of the USA and politics. I was surprised at the depth of knowledge many of these folks had about our country as well as their interest in our politics. I had to endure their jokes and criticism of the USA, and especially about some of our presidents. They were carefully watching my reaction, but I just let them talk and tried to answer their questions. Trying to explain to some frustrated Europeans why George W. Bush was going to win or explain the popularity of Donald Trump, were both interesting conversations. I am not sure what the reasons were for all of this, but most of the people there loved Bill Clinton and Barack Obama, and they really did not like George H. W. Bush or Donald Trump. It could have been Bush's invasion of Kuwait or Trump's attitude of "USA first," I don't know. They loved that a man of color could be president, and they loved everything about Bill Clinton. However, Serbian folks did not—since the bombing of Serbia and eventual capture of Milošević took place under his direction.

I knew that my time was coming to leave Croatia, and I needed to find a college that wanted to hire me. I had conducted several research projects that were published during this time. I enjoyed living in central Europe so much that I thought I would send my résumé to several universities, to see whether anything would turn up. Eventually, I was offered a job in the Czech Republic, with the Faculty of Physical Culture, Palacký University, as well as a part-time job at a private management school in Trieste, Italy. The former one turned out to be a full-time job; the latter one, although very lucrative, was a part-time, one-day lecture that occurred once a year. (The one-day lecture in Italy was equal to an entire salary for a month in the Czech Republic.)

My main job was in Olomouc at Palacký University, College of Physical Culture, and I thought they wanted me for the Department of Recreation; however, eventually, I realized they wanted me to be part of their Erasmus program, which was in English. I did this for twelve years. I tried everything to get into their own system; I even took the time to become a "docent." Even after becoming a docent (associate professor), this still did not work; it never worked out for me to have my own PhD students. This confusing situation became a frustration, and so, eventually I knew I needed to leave. My contract had finished, and it was a convenient time for me to go.

My time there was wonderful in its own unique way. I had the opportunity to teach hundreds of students in this Erasmus program from all over Europe. Also, I was conducting research there in the Czech Republic. This became a confusing and frustrating time and eventually my contract with the college was not renewed. Usually in the USA, we are fairly free to express our opinion; however, where I was working, this was not the case. When I became too outspoken on a certain topic at the college (though I don't know), I crossed some line, and soon my contract ended and was not renewed. Also their system of formal education is so different for me; it is free for students who qualify, there are long periods for exams (like six weeks), undergraduates have to do some mandatory research before they finish, failing a class is no big deal (you did not pay for it), and there are strict oral exams at the end for each graduate, which takes weeks of time. Also, you go to the college to learn; there are not many student clubs or extra-curricular activities if any. In contrast, the University of Georgia has almost three hundred student clubs and organizations.

Some positive experiences at work at the university in the Czech Republic were traveling to other schools for interaction and lectures, getting money to go to conferences, having the freedom to research, and my boss helping me with salary to pay for the university dorm. There was a special relationship with a few of my PhD students who invited me into their homes, and I was able to meet and spend time with their families. I enjoyed being able to do some unique research in this part of the world on topics such as gardening, dancing, skiing, walking, and traveling.

There were several unique aspects of this university, and one of them was the activity-oriented program—such as ski school, winter camp, lifelong learning camp, or bicycle camp. I attended a few of these where they would take their students on a one-week or two-week program of learning how to ski, bike, or create games, and this was fun-oriented education with the students and teachers. This does not happen in the USA. I had a nice office at the Faculty of Physical Culture, and I enjoyed time with my colleagues; they were so nice to me, and sometimes, I would be able to help them with something concerning the English language. I also offered classes for my colleagues on publishing, ethics in research, or qualitative research, and I had some positive responses from this.

Scenario. Fall of 2007. "Yes, Donald, I am sarcastic and bitter at the life we were given," he said with a smile. "You see, this building, our office, and all of this part of the university, housed Russian soldiers during the Czechoslovakian days. The airport," he said, pointing out the window (at now a recreational airport), "was the airbase for the Russian army, for the entire Czechoslovakia. For some reason, Olomouc was their center during this time of Czechoslovakia. They occupied us! They did liberate us from the Nazis, but then, maybe their forty-year reign was worse. My parents were even communist to try to fit into the system. My dream in life was to have a pair of blue jeans and to listen to the Beatles. We lost a lot of time, so yes, I am bitter." Later when I thought about my office mate, and the things he said, the more

I realized I came from a country or area so separated from anything like this. I had grown up in a safe and happy situation where there was order, color, and everything was under a rainbow—and worse, I never even knew it.

Inside every school are some of those interesting and unusual places. In my elementary school there was this auditorium, and on either side of the stage were small rooms, and they became the depository of leftover objects that were fascinating to see. In the same way, travel, if you slow down, will always show some interesting things. In the allegory of the tortoise and the hare, supposedly everyone thinks the hare will win the race, but ultimately, it is the very slow tortoise. If you are going fast, you will not see in detail, you don't have time to meet people, and you can be dangerous trying "to get there." The best travel is the opposite of a race, where the winner is not the fastest one. Come Walk with Me is an international walking program based on simply walking with someone and finishing the walk. Time is not the issue. This is more my style of sport; come with me and let's explore the world.

Some Unique Aspects of Life in the Czech Republic

While I was working at Palacký University in Olomouc, Czech Republic, I noticed there was a school newspaper. I went to the editor and suggested that I write something about the way I see life in the Czech Republic. He thought it over, and we came up with the idea that I would write something interesting about living in the Czech Republic, and he would translate it. He put five of these paragraphs in the university paper. One version is in English, and one is in Czech. I have placed the exact five short paragraphs I wrote here.

The subjects are the following: mushrooming, how it works in the post office and grocery store, driving with lights on, weekly public announcements, and the cafeteria at the college.

I am hearing voices...

I was in my office, minding my work, paying attention to necessary details—All of a sudden, a siren, or gong, then a voice started speaking loudly. I knew it was not the voice of an angel or even God Himself—because I did not understand a word of it—but it was loud and everywhere! I could not imagine what was going on—my colleagues at the office pointed to a previously unseen speaker outside of the building from where this voice was arising. Now once a month I am used to the drill. First the siren, then some type of gong, and then some speech. Most of my colleagues just shake their head and say it is something left over from the last era in Czech. I can imagine they are saying things like—Ok fellow Olomouc people—get busy, look smart, and love your neighbor. Or, maybe they are saying—be nice when you are walking down the street, pay your taxes, and watch out for the bad guy. Or, they are saying support the ice hockey team, or football team, or come to the town center to support the local businesses! Regardless, I think it is a grand idea. Someone that we should import around the world!

Donald N. Roberson, Jr.
odborný asistent, FTK

Mensa

So, I am going to the cafeteria to eat lunch. I had just arrived in Olomouc. I walk straight up to the line in the restaurant and start to point at certain food. And I motion for them, to remove the covers, so I can see what to choose. I knew instantly I was doing something wrong. There was a great deal of shouting and pointing and speaking in Czech. I really could not imagine what the problem was. Here I was, hungry, standing in a cafeteria, and all I wanted was for the lady to put some food on my tray and let me go. I showed them I had Czech money! Then one of them takes me over to some box, it looks like a juke-box in USA—where you play music. She starts to hit something on the screen. Eventually I look into the faces of the curious crowd and say—'Does anyone here speak English.' Someone came to my rescue—shock of shocks—that black box, was some giant menu for me to order food on. I could not believe that I couldn't just walk up to the line of food, see what they have, point it out, and pay! Then I was told I would have to order food over this computer if I ever wanted to eat in this cafeteria. Amazing how controlled is the choice and the use of the food in the mensas. Quite dictatorial response to food—however, probably there is not much waste! Well, I have a lot to learn!

Donald N. Roberson, Jr.
odborný asistent, FTK

Mushrooming

One interesting difference in USA and central Europe and especially Czech is the entire topic of mushrooming. Basically we are told to stay away – we are forbidden to touch – and most people are stepping on them or kicking them. I had to restrain myself as I was led one day while walking a distant path in north Moravia, and my companions all of sudden started to point, they were smiling, laughing, and even running deeper into the woods. I could not imagine what spell, or incantation had led them astray – and they came back with scores of mushrooms. A few years later, one father of a friend, invited me to join him on his mushroom hunting, I thought okay, I am going to get in the nature and learn how to do this. Four hours later, we emerged from the woods, completely tired, with a rainbow color of toadstools in all sorts of sizes and shapes. Then I began to watch my friend to clean this collection of fungi. He was sort of transfixed into another world of happiness and attention. Later we ate some amazing soup from these mushrooms. I was bracing myself to fall over at any time, or perhaps I would die in my sleep, I could see my mother's finger wagging at me from all the way across the ocean. Or, maybe there was going to start some hallucinogenic mind trip as a result of the mushroom. Actually it was all very nice, learning about the forest, walking up and down, smelling the forest air and the earthy tones of the mushrooms, and I slept very well! One thing for sure, when my American friends come here, I am going to take them mushroom hunting!

Donald N. Roberson, Jr.
odborný asistent, FTK

Post Office and Grocery

Going to the 'Posta' one can accomplish so much. Not only the mailing of letters and packages, but also the paying of bills! There is even various gifts to buy, such as Pat and Matt, books, even candy. But the best idea for me is the orderly way of giving numbers and everyone waiting in turn. I just press ,universal' and it works each time. In contrast in the USA, the financially troubled post office only deals with mailing letters and packages. There may be a few other services concerning the government, but not the paying of your bills.

Even better ideas are found in your grocery stores. First, the grocery cart must have a coin deposit. This motivates the shopper to return the cart. In the USA grocery carts are a problem and must be constantly gathered by the workers. Second, the return of glass bottles is so easy! Just put it in the machine and eventually you get a receipt. I have never seen anything like this in USA, we could use it. But we do have something you don't—someone to help you put your groceries in a bag—the bag boy! And if you need help with these bags, they will help you take them to your car.

Donald N. Roberson, Jr.
odborný asistent, FTK

Turn on your lights!

I was told 'be prepared' when I decided to take a job in the Czech Republic! One thing, my friend said, Czech people are not so friendly. Well, I thought, I had lived in the former Yugoslavia for seven years, and after surviving those downcast frowns and negative thoughts, I thought for sure I can handle Czech people.

But, to my surprise, when I drove around the town, I saw a different side of Czech people. They were friendly, even friendly, in a cute sort of way. They would see me coming in my car, they would look at me, put their hand together, and make some unique movement. Sort of like holding your hand out and touching all your fingers together. I thought well, I know now this is a friendly place, and they have a special hand greeting to wave when you are driving. Perhaps this is the physical way to say Ahoj!

And then one colleague got into the car with me and said turn on your lights, Donald. And, if you don't turn your lights on, usually people will give you a little sign like—and to my disappointment he made that same sign.

Oh well, I do miss the friendly waves since I now have turned my car lights on. But I am safer, it's a good idea to drive with your lights on, and the Czech folks can return to their own life, instead of worrying about trying to get me to turn my lights on.

Donald N. Roberson, Jr.
odborný asistent, FTK

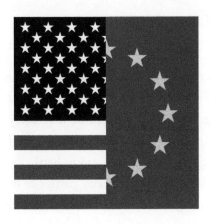

Chapter Twenty-Two:

More Comparisons between Life Here and Life There

After graduation, the graduate looks back, reflects, and remembers certain aspects of the school. They may see them more clearly and may long for some of the aspects of the school, or they may wish to forget others. Also in travel, or living abroad, you may continue to remember some of the lessons you learned, the difficult situations, and the great adventures of your travel experience. Although I love the USA and Georgia (where I am from), there are certain things I really miss and became used to when traveling. What do I miss about central Europe?

Atmosphere. It is August 2021. I am sitting here in Zagreb, Croatia, at the recreation area called Jarun. It is a very large city park with water for swimming and playing, lots of playgrounds, space for rowing competitions, bicycle paths, walking paths, even a small nudist beach, a skating path, and lots of restaurants and cafés. At this moment, behind me is a group of older folks who come here every Tuesday to have lunch and sing. There is a guitar and an accordion. I miss open parks, the singing with guitars, the casual atmosphere, the lingering meals. I was fortunate to attend many birthday parties or other get-togethers, where everyone was gathered around a table covered with food and local wine, and the essence of the get-together was singing with the guitar—a beautiful experience.

Pubs. Most every neighborhood in central Europe has a local pub. The word for pub in Czech is "hospoda," similar to hospital! And, it is like a large den, with children and dogs, everyone sitting, talking, and laughing. Some play games, others sing, some drink local beers, and many drink a local version of Coca-Cola (Kofola), or tea. And sometimes you see two people, with heads close to each other, in a very serious conversation. In the evening, many folks do not stay at home; they go to the pub and sit for an hour or two. Yet at the same time, there are many folks who never go to the pub, especially those with small children.

Parks. In this part of Europe, there is a great importance placed on public space. So there are parks with benches, tables, even concrete Ping-Pong tables. Especially in the larger cities, the parks are often crowded. This may be due to housing in crowded buildings and the fact that most of the people live within the city.

Café shops. Going for a coffee is indeed a ritual. You go to the café and get the real thing made in those big machines like you see in Starbucks. Small coffee, yet strong, served with a glass of water, and you make it last thirty minutes. There are no refills. If you want another, you pay. But it is a huge part of life. Everyone loves to go to the café, and they are everywhere. It is in the café where most of life occurs, where most decisions are made, and where most relationships take place. The Starbucks company, based on this concept of coffee with the Italian coffee machines, brought this to the USA in the '70s. This concept was based on folks traveling in Europe and seeing the coffee shops, and thinking, *We do not have this in the USA.*

Local churches with services and songs in their native language. It's an interesting experience to go to a church in another country and hear the service in another language. You learn about the creativity of God, languages, and people. It helps one to go beyond one's own perspective of a home church. This is very easy to do—you can search for a church in the area where you are going and just join them. Usually, I will bring my journal and my own Bible and I will read on my own and enjoy the service with them. I walk away understanding more of "God so loved the World" (John 3:16, New American Standard Bible).

Bicycle trails. There are many bicycle trails all through Europe. In some large cities, bikes will have their own stop signs, even traffic signals. Now, in many large cities, they have bikes everywhere for rent. Some of the bicycles you rent in person; others, there may be an app to use on your mobile phone, or even a credit card machine. It's the best way to get around. Further, in small towns and villages, people of all ages and types ride bicycles everywhere. It's not a matter of recreation; it is rather an economic need. They go to the market, or school, on their bike. I have seen many older women dressed all in black, scarf on their heads, riding the bikes with their baskets full of groceries, coming home in the middle of the busy road. They were comfortable, determined, and owned the road. Within the last few years, the biking situation has been changing, especially with electric bicycles.

Walking streets and town squares without cars. Many towns in Europe, even small towns, have a center in the town without cars. It is completely pedestrianized, and the roads are for people to walk, or sometimes there are cafés in the streets. It makes for a relaxed center of town where people can leisurely enjoy the town. Some of these centers are huge and full of beautiful statues, benches, and fountains. Some of my favorite town centers are Olomouc and Prague in the Czech Republic, Krakow in Poland, and Zagreb in Croatia. This creates an atmosphere where there is always something to do. Just go to the center of the town, sit in an outdoor café, and enjoy the ambience.

Beautiful buildings and architecture. Europe is famous for its buildings, many of which are hundreds of years old, some even a thousand years old—buildings with creative art and architecture. These buildings were built because the area was controlled by a ruler or king who could order some type of building, whereas in many countries, such as in the USA, there was nothing. Buildings were made of lumber or the easiest way. So there lingers in Europe many castles, churches, and city centers that I would recommend for you to see, including, for example, Venice!

`Adding to this, it is even easier to gain acceptance into many countries because English is considered a universal language, especially in academics, sports, and business. There was a book that came out in the '50s called *The Ugly American.* This book essentially describes the way governments with power can negatively impact other places. We have to prove to those around us we are not "ugly." For example, if I am doing something that is offensive to them, then I can easily lose this undue respect. Or, they may make a joke about the USA, or the president, or ask my opinion about something controversial in the USA. And, if they want to criticize me or the USA, I just let it happen and try to listen to them.

Cultural life—opera, ballet, symphony, music. During the fourth to twelfth grades, I took piano lessons, so I had become somewhat familiar with the classical style of music. Adding to this, in high

This building can represent the thousands of interiors across Europe that are beautifully decorated. It is quite rare to see something like this in the USA. This is actually the ceiling in one of the older music halls in Prague, Czech Republic.

school, I attended one summer academic program that offered various cultural activities. And during the time I lived in Athens, Georgia, the university would sponsor concerts from people around the world, and I volunteered to be an usher there—but I had never been around this culture in a regular way. When I first lived in Zagreb, there were regular ongoing programs of opera, ballet, and the symphony, and I slowly got into it. For me, the opera was and still is a slow learning experience (leaning toward boredom). I enjoyed most the ballet, and also the symphony (where there are no words involved). In the Czech Republic, it was also very much a part of everyday life—the opera, the symphony, the ballet, and other types of traditional music. Even in my town of Olomouc, of one hundred thousand people, there was a full opera, ballet, and symphony. And, if I went two hours away to Prague, it was a world-class collection of culture. Because I went so often, I would try to find a "stand-up" seat, or other cheaper seat, and many times I could; however, that also became its own interesting experience to stand up for two hours of serious classical music. Depending on where you sit, you can pay from thirty-five to one hundred euro for a seat. If you stand up, the entrance is around five euro. I recommend that you visit the Vienna State Opera, the Golden Hall or "Musikverein," and in Prague, the State Opera, the National Theatre, the Rudolfinum, and the Estates Theatre. I was many times in all of these. (In Vienna, when the State Opera house was built, the emperor wanted anyone to be able to go, so he had them create a stand-up section, which was way up in the ceiling of the opera house. Today, you have to stand in line for about two to four hours to get these tickets.)

Football/hooligans. I went often to football/fudbal matches, or as we say in the USA, soccer, with huge crowds, equal to any large college football or NFL game you may have seen; however, one difference is a group called the "fan club." Each team has its own "fan club." This group often gets together, or organizes themselves, and will learn songs, have nicknames, and support the team. However, once they get violent, and they may, they have another name: "hooligans." This group of folks are usually younger men. They take their shirts off, and they are ready for a game—and a fight. In many stadiums, this group of folks will have to sit in a separate place, often screened in by some wiring, or fencing, and they are often escorted to and from the stadium by police. I have stumbled upon many fans of fudbal teams, waiting for their game, while visiting other European towns. Walking down one street, you would see hundreds of the fans with their same color shirts sitting in cafés and pubs drinking glass after glass of pivo, and then on the other side of the street is the other team's fans, doing the same. Starring at one another, comparing each other, laughing and pointing, and all of sudden, they are caught up in something important, significant, and meaningful.

Ice hockey. In the Czech Republic, the most popular sport is ice hockey. It is for sure one of the most demanding sports, like playing football on ice. It is so demanding that the players will be replaced every one to two minutes. Yes, of course, we have ice hockey in the USA, but it is somewhat limited to aspects of the NHL. In the Czech Republic, almost every village had a large ice rink for skating and time for hockey.

Atheists. I met many atheists while living in central Europe. And maybe most of my friends and colleagues there would readily identify as atheist. Sometimes I thought that they really meant they don't go to some church because I know they had a spiritual interest. One of my students, after I had given all of them an English version of the New Testament, said to me, "Mr. Donald, you must understand we are atheist, and we are proud to be." Keep in mind, however, that the churches are full, and I attended several different types of Protestant churches as well. It was interesting to be around everyday folks who were proud to be atheist. They seemed to regard religion as a good luck charm for folks who needed something like that.

Cold and snow. Being from South Georgia, living in north Europe was a very new experience. And, I grew to really like the cold, the snow. I eventually had my own downhill and cross-country skis and ice skates. I participated as much as I could; one small downhill slope was only a fifteen-minute drive, and larger ones were one to two hours away. Cross-country trails were everywhere in all of the forests. And, in Olomouc, the ice-skating rink for ice hockey was open often for public ice-skating.

Public transportation. I enjoyed immensely the public system of travel. When I first started living in Zagreb, we learned how to use this system. It is a city of around one million, and there are electric "trams," train cars, taking people to every place you would need to go. Maybe at the most you would need to walk ten minutes. And if you are venturing further out, there is a train or bus system going to every village. It is somehow different when you are waiting or riding with others, often strangers. Vastly different from a car parked in your garage, where you enter from your house, adjust your own temperature, or music, and place what you want in the backseat or trunk. I used public transportation for twenty years and took it for granted; it took some adjusting when I returned to the USA, and I realized how the car is so individual, so comfortable, but maybe isolating.

Medical system. Everyone works in central Europe. And when you receive your pay, there is a deduction for medical and retirement. You are presented with a medical card, and when you enter the hospital, there is no mention of money. You present your card, and they try to heal whatever is ailing you. If you have some special situation, then you may have to pay more, or even go to another country. But for most folks, the basic medicine and treatments—including pregnancy, sickness, surgery, MRI exams, X-rays—are all paid. There is no one meeting with you trying to get your money or payments. The intent of the medical system is to keep the population healthy. One doctor friend said to me, "Donald, don't complain, your country chose medicine for profit. We have medicine to serve the public." There are many misconceptions about this type of medicine; regardless, I found it effective and equal to ours. In addition, if you can imagine, there are no high salaries for medical doctors. Their salary is very similar to others—almost $1,000 a month.

Variety of trees. Having grown up in semitropical South Georgia, USA, I appreciated seeing a new variety of trees in northern Europe.

Different varieties of oak, tulip, pines, conifers, and hemlock were very nice to be around. I love to be outside in all the variety of weather, so the nature in this area was so appealing to discover.

Grandparents. It is the Baka (grandma) who rules the country. People don't move around in this area as much as in the USA. And, because of this, the grandparents, or actually all four of them, are close by. They are the ones who take care of the family while the parents are working. Some will have food ready every day for their children and grandchildren. Some will retrieve their grandchildren from school and spend time with them until the parents of the grandchild come home. And, sometimes, they are all living in the same house. They are an integral part of the daily life of the family and are really happy to be involved in this. Babysitting is not a normal situation. If grandparents are not close by or accessible, then you are with your children until they are independent.

Dubravko

February of 1994. I met Dubravko while he was a student at the engineering college. We had asked if we could give some English classes in their department of English. They were happy to have some native English speakers. And we asked the students to fill out a card if they would like to meet with us. Dubravko did, as previously he had met some Americans with a Christian program who were playing his team in baseball. Dubravko was on a baseball team in Croatia, and he even had a pitching machine at his home! He lived in a nearby village not far from Zagreb. I met with him a few times, and eventually, he came to our weekly get-togethers. I met his family, and his grandmother, who also lived with them. Their house contained three levels, and it had a flower garden with a barbeque area. They were friendly with all their neighbors, and one neighbor would often come over every day for a friendly drink and hello with Dubravko's father. Dubravko's grandmother, a widow, lived with them. She wore completely solid black, and she was so sweet and kind, and she helped out the family as much as she could with cooking, cleaning, and gardening. I remember at that time on the upstairs patio, it was covered with shelled corn, showing their ties to this rural area. They had a large garden plot a ten-minute drive away, where they grew a lot of vegetables. Because Dubravko lived within fifteen miles of the university, he could not stay in a dormitory, but he continued to live at home during his university years.

My friend's grandmother proudly showing me some of her sewing. She had become a refugee during the Yugoslav Wars, having to leave her family home in eastern Slavonia.

He was interested in many aspects of American life, cars, and music. One of his hobbies was to convert regular cars into convertibles! He often discussed with me how he wanted to live abroad. And now, he is living and working with his family in another country.

Marko

I met Marko while playing basketball with students. An excellent athlete, and an engineering student, he was friendly and spoke English well. So, I found out where he lived and I came to visit him in the dorm. (At that time you could just walk into the dorms.) And he also had a side business selling CDs. I remember buying *Space Jam* from him (it is still playing).

We played several sporting activities together, and I found out he was a serious rower. More interesting, his hometown, Subotica, is in an independent Serbian province called Vojvodina, which was an autonomous area of Serbia, north of Belgrade, where a lot of Croatians lived. (Did you understand all of that?) He had to drive for six to eight hours to get to the university. I joined him once in his town of Subotica—a small, beautiful town in this interesting area. His family lived in a rural area outside the town. His mother is a devout Catholic and very active in church activities, and she pleads with her family to follow the right way. During the Yugoslav Wars, it was a difficult time for his family, being in Serbia. He was tough and bright, and after university, he started to work in the Vienna area. I visited him many times in Vienna. He and his family have done well there. He has continued with rowing and has won many medals.

This is a typical house in a village in central Europe. Notice the painting on the outside of a local scene as well as the well-tended garden in cultivation. There is often a basement, and usually Mother and Father are on the ground floor, and one of their children lives with their family on the second floor.

Chapter Twenty-Three:
Conclusion

My generation and older—I salute you—I honor you.

Most of the folks I have described in this book are about thirty years or so younger than I am, and at some time, they may have been one of my students. Most of them I met around the university. If it was possible, I wanted to meet their family, parents, and grandparents, to see their life in their home area. When I would be with one of their parents or grandparents, I was literally in awe of them and the situations that they had endured. Wars, communism, Nazis—everything was literally taken from them, and they had to fit into the new system. Both of these countries where I lived, Croatia and the Czech Republic, had previously done very well. However, they had been the victim of bigger powers and events changing their politics and lives. They all seemed to survive these difficult times. Even though the new governments after World War II had confiscated everything they had, they had somehow forged ahead, adapted, and adjusted. Most of them had created a comfortable home for their family despite this new and confusing world order. Sometimes, if there was a translator, I would ask them politely to share with me about life during these times. One interesting aspect of this group of people is the notion that they had lost a lot of time during the Nazi and Communist regimes. In Prague, there is a very large metronome, swinging back and forth, as if reminding the people of how much time had been lost. (Interestingly, this metronome is standing in the very spot where previously there had been the world's largest statue of Stalin.) It seems to me, on reflection, that because of this sense of lost time, and with social media, seeing the lifestyle in the West, people here, especially young ones, are in a constant frenzy of busyness, perhaps trying to make up for this lost time. But I also know folks in the USA who also are "overly" busy, one writer called it "the tyranny of the urgent"—so perhaps this is a human condition showing the importance of free time and a proper perspective of rest and leisure.

Graduation from the School of Travel

In some situations, school can become very comfortable. One may really enjoy the learning, the people, the teachers, and the activities. But the purpose of school is to prepare the student to leave. They should finish school with skills they would not have learned otherwise, and they should be able to go into the world in order to work and hopefully make the world a better place.

Eventually this happened to me. Maybe I was not ready to leave "the school of travel," but I knew that it was coming. Similar to a senior in high school, who is getting bored, making friends with teachers instead of fellow students, and looking to what is in the future, I received the notice that it was time for me also to leave this particular part of my school of travel. I had several goodbye parties and ended my time in central Europe. Some of the main lessons I learned during this school of travel are the following.

Making friends with locals. In contrast to most travel and tourism, when one is living in the area, it is so much easier to get to know the local folks. Everyone likes to know someone from a different country, and it makes the world a friendlier place. If I went to a particular store or location in the town, I would try to get to know the people there. Always speak something (like good morning) in their language, and then politely ask, "Do you speak English?" (And don't be surprised at the responses you will get.) This is possible on all trips, short or long. Just be friendly to others and see what happens.

Getting to know the area where I lived. I wanted to feel like a local, so I attempted to acquaint myself with the area around me. This often included buying a map and experimenting by driving in the area as well as taking public transport. I would put up a map on the wall of the area, and if someone came to see me, I would put a pin in the area where they lived. I would look for books about the local area in English or maps, and of course, now there is information on the internet.

Learning to be happy where I am. One of the most valuable lessons in life is to learn to be happy where you are. One of the first people to state this, an itinerant preacher, wrote, "I have learned to be content in whatever circumstances I am" (Philippians 4:11). We are taught all of our lives that you need to be at home and around your family and friends to be happy. However, it is very liberating, while you are traveling, to see that you can also be happy anywhere. This is so important because it allows you to enjoy where you are, to learn more about the people in this area, and to be focused on your activity—rather than wishing you were somewhere else. Home is where you are; home becomes wherever you are. This is one of the great lessons of life.

Keeping up with family and friends at home. Although I was focused on being in the present and the current moment, there were people that I did want to keep up with. In a normal situation, people often "bury" those who leave, or forget them until they return. Today it is easier than ever with the computer or internet programs such as Skype, WhatsApp, FaceTime, and Facebook, or simply by texting. I refuse to listen to anyone's excuses about time when it is so easy to speak to anyone around the world for a few minutes.

In contrast, I will tell you about one experience in Bucharest, Romania. In the summer of 1992, which I have previously described, I had promised my mother I would try to call from there at least once. We were told to go to the center of communication for Bucharest. It was early evening, yet already dark (they were not using streetlights since the revolution), and we went to this large antiquated building. We all went, about eight of us, trying to call home for a few minutes. We stood in line, and seriously, it was like the United Nations had gathered. It looked as if each person of every tribe and tongue was there. We stood in line, I gave the person my home phone number, and I paid her for ten minutes. I went inside a booth and the person I gave the money to created the call. Thankfully my mom was there, and although it sounded like we were far apart, we were able to hear each other. In contrast, today over the internet, you can call and talk almost for free. It is no longer an excuse not to keep up with someone. While I was in the Czech Republic, I was sure my mother would not be around much longer, so I decided that I would call her every day on Skype. It took some getting used to, and I had to explain to my ma that we would talk every day for ten minutes, just tell me what you are doing. It made a huge difference in our relationship, and I felt she was close.

Classes I failed. One class I failed was fitting into the culture and the society, mainly because I did not become fluent in the language. This certainly limits the conversations you can have, and only folks who wanted to speak English would spend time with me. This is even worse in the USA. In most situations, we do not even tolerate another language. We are not used to it. Another mistake is that I offered too many suggestions for improvement at work. There were many aspects of their education that were very different from the Western perspective. These included oral exams, students not paying any fees, research for undergraduate students, a physical test for incoming students, and the way they treated PhD students. I was often vocal about my thoughts concerning these issues as well as how to change them. As with every successful worker, I should have shown more responsibility by accepting more of their ideas. If you are working for someone, you must fit into their ideas and programs.

Knowledge of geography and history. I can describe the geography of former Yugoslavia, current Croatia, the Adriatic Sea, and the coastline of Croatia. I can explain details about the Czech Republic and Slovakia. I know about the conflicts and situations of former Yugoslavia as well as Czechoslovakia. This experiential learning naturally took place because of traveling in the area, the hundreds of conversations I had, as well as reading.

How to make new friends. Friendships take time, patience, understanding. To make a new friend, a true one, it is not based on similar looks or ideas; it is based on spending time with each other, doing activities together, accepting each other, and keeping in touch. It's very special when this occurs within families; however, the amazing potential within any culture is the possibility to make a friend. It's easier now than ever with the internet, social media, and email. Many people eventually become grandparents, and often the friendships will "suffer" because of this enticing little wonder in one's life. Just keep this in mind when your international friends take on these new roles.

Willingness to partake in new adventures. When you live and travel in another place, you must become a partaker of new activities like going home with someone and being around their family, learning to speak a different language, going by their rules rather than the ones you were used to, going with them on some suggested outing (and you have no idea what it will be), as well as daily activities such as washing, cooking, or eating in a new way.

Lingering Thoughts about Travel

Travel writer and creator of travel experiences—I refer to someone I have read for many years—Rick Steves, said: "We travel all the way to Europe to enjoy differences—to become temporary locals. You'll experience frustrations. Certain truths that we find 'God-given' or 'self-evident,' like cold beer, ice in drinks, bottomless cups of coffee, and bigger being better, are suddenly not so true. One of the benefits of travel is the eye-opening realization that there are logical, civil, and even better alternatives. The fact that Americans treat time as a commodity can lead to frustrations when dealing with other cultures. For instance, while an American 'spends' or 'wastes' time, a French person merely 'passes' it. A willingness to go local (and at a local tempo) ensures that you'll enjoy a full dose of European hospitality." (Steves, Rick. 2000. *Rick Steves' France, Belgium and the Netherlands*. Santa Fe, New Mexico: John Muir Publications.)

Traveling is much better than tourism. The longer you stay, the better; the smaller the group, the better. Become your own tour guide or ask others. Meet local people and do what they are doing. Interact with others in the same way you would if you were a guest in their house. Travel is simple and easy, and there are a host of people who want to help you because of the financial prospects of tourism. If you check with the State Department on the safeness of travel, then all else should be okay. Learn about the geography and history of the area. Go beyond your travel companions and their funny stories while traveling to genuinely meet with local folks and have them explain about their life. Try to do something, volunteer somewhere, or create something if possible. Find some common ground with others—such as church, civic group, family, work, or hobbies. Write a story and put it in your local paper. Travel with a journal to write down your thoughts and ideas. Be available to make friends, folks who may want to keep up with you, and even visit; it is so easy today with the internet. Travel does not have to be far. Explore your backyard. Explore your area—drive on every road in your county. Take time to visit new groups, visit other churches, and meet other people.

About the Author

The author at one of his favorite places, the UNESCO-designated area of
Kroměříž, Czech Republic. This is the formal gardens of the former archbishop.
Europe is well known for its manicured gardens and ornate palaces.

Donald (Donny) N. Roberson, Jr. currently lives in Berrien County, Georgia. After high school, he attended the University of Georgia. During this time, he became active in Campus Crusade for Christ (now called Cru) and decided to join their staff, resulting in a thirty-year career with this Christian student organization. Also while in college, he worked each summer at Rock Eagle 4-H Camp, where he learned various aspects of recreation, team building, and education. During his time with Cru, Roberson spent almost every summer in unique and beautiful locations—including Yellowstone, Colorado, and Lake Tahoe, California. Eventually, he was asked to help the program get started in central Europe—Zagreb, Croatia. These experiences helped to lay a foundation for knowledge of travel.

Eventually, Roberson earned a PhD from the University of Georgia and then returned to central Europe for another fifteen years. In 2007, he was hired at Palacký University, in Olomouc, Czech Republic, where he remained for twelve years. He continued research in this area and eventually became a docent/associate professor in public health and recreation. Today, Roberson continues to be involved in writing and research. You can find Roberson's research via Google Scholar. Roberson welcomes your comments at dnrobersonjr@gmail.com.

A free ebook edition is available with the purchase of this book.

To claim your free ebook edition:

1. Visit MorganJamesBOGO.com
2. Sign your name CLEARLY in the space
3. Complete the form and submit a photo of the entire copyright page
4. You or your friend can download the ebook to your preferred device

Morgan James
BOGO™

A **FREE** ebook edition is available for you or a friend with the purchase of this print book.

CLEARLY SIGN YOUR NAME ABOVE

Instructions to claim your free ebook edition:
1. Visit MorganJamesBOGO.com
2. Sign your name CLEARLY in the space above
3. Complete the form and submit a photo of this entire page
4. You or your friend can download the ebook to your preferred device

Print & Digital Together Forever.

Snap a photo

Free ebook

Read anywhere